To Beverly
Enjoy!

BALLET VIGNETTES

ARNOLD L. HASKELL

THE ALBYN PRESS

42 FREDERICK STREET EDINBURGH 2

First published 1948

THE ALBYN PRESS
42 Frederick Street
Edinburgh, 2

DEDICATED TO
VERA VOLKOVA
who is not committed by the opinions
but who so often delights me when
she shares them.

A.L.H.

Printed in Great Britain by
Scottish County Press
Dalkeith

CONTENTS

ILLUSTRATIONS

CHAPTER I — THE DANCER

1.—CRITICAL STANDARDS

It is never easy to write critically on the subject of dancers. How to convey the excitement communicated by some great performance, or the particular quality of some dancer?

There is a science as well as an art of dancing, but to write in scientific jargon is not only to be clumsy but to make oneself unintelligible to the majority. Comparisons, however odious, are inevitable in criticism. If the reader is unfamiliar with the dancers compared, then the whole comparison misfires. But the most serious difficulty of all is that any writing on the younger contemporaries tends to date with a disconcerting rapidity. In the early years of the century a dancer did not appear until she was formed, while to-day she is formed in front of her public. With a dancer the formative period for physical as well as psychological reasons is more critical than with any other artist. How is she going to react to what is really hard physical labour? In a season or two she may have grown too fat or too tall. The critic may talk of a Greuze and find himself confronted by a Rubens. In such a case he is more apt to blame the dancer than himself for his premature enthusiasm. Yet to hedge on all occasions is both dull and discouraging. The critic writes as much for the dancer as for her public.

Before deciding whether to publish these studies the writer went through his press records of the past twenty years. He found there enthusiastic notices of the first appearances of Markova, Danilova, Nikitina, Pearl Argyle and the whole Rambert group, Baronova, Toumanova, Riabouchinska, Fonteyn, May and Brae. Even if in some cases the praise was not sufficiently tempered by criticism, the record seemed a justification for this collection of dancers' vignettes.

It is necessary first, however, to explain the critic's point of view, his use of certain words and his choice of certain dancers.

Let us take the last point right away; it is easy to dismiss in a very few words. The choice is and can only be a personal one. Certain dancers are easy to discuss, as much on account of their faults as of their virtues, others leave one little

5

to say; maybe on account of those virtues. There are such things as endearing faults and cold almost mathematical virtues. Omissions do not convey a lack of admiration; this is no book of graded box-office favourites.

The first thing the reader will rightly want to know is what are the author's standards. Is there an absolute standard of perfection even in the interpretation of a single rôle, let us say Odette-Odile in *Swan Lake?* There might be such a standard geometrically speaking. But even if a machine could be found by which to measure technique, it would tell us precisely nothing. Differences of physique, personality, temperament, musical interpretation and dramatic interpretation are all things that cannot possibly be measured. Moreover one cannot measure the critic's own personal reaction to such things since they are largely conditioned by his taste, knowledge and experience.

I often ask myself what mental process actually goes on when watching a dancer for the first time in a familiar rôle. The immediate reaction seems to be a call on memory and experience. How did Trefilova dance *Swan Lake* or *The Sleeping Princess,* Pavlova *Giselle,* Karsavina *Le Spectre de la Rose?* Trefilova, Pavlova, Karsavina—these then are the standards of a man of my generation. They are high standards since the dancers evoked were produced by a perfect system, developed gradually and in close contact with the creators of the classic rôles. Also the audiences before whom they made their debûts largely consisted of connoisseurs and contained such keen critics as Volinsky, Svetloff and Levinson. Yet in invoking such standards there are many necessary adjustments to be made. There is firstly the danger of a hardening of critical arteries and a lack of sympathy for the present generation. At some time or other every individual ceases to react to the new and looks back on the old with an acute nostalgia. The important thing for the critic is to realise when that time has come and then to make a graceful exit.

Technique in every art develops enormously in extent if not in quality. Let us take as an example those notorious thirty-two *fouettés* in *Swan Lake.* Kchesinska was the first Russian dancer to learn them from her master Legat's observation of the Italian Pierrina Legnani. Therefore in her technical repertoire and in the eyes of her public they were always in the nature of a " stunt." Pavlova and other great dancers of the time never learnt them. To-day they have become almost a commonplace, especially as performed by the pupils of that great teacher, Olga Preobrajenska. They are therefore no longer a stunt but a part of the current language of dancing. In some respects the good average dancers of the past would date if we saw them to-day. I have noticed that in comparing photographs of the original Sylphides with those of to-day.

Another danger in evoking memory, quite apart from the tricks of exaggeration that memory plays, is the intrusion of the personality of the great dancer of yesterday. The uncritical often talk of a " second Pavlova," where a second Pavlova, if possible, would be less significant than a plaster case of Donatello's

6

David. Already Pavlova has made one rôle, *The Dying Swan,* so very much her own that no dancer in her right state of mind would dare perform it.

Let us by all means evoke standards but only so long as we allow for the change and development of technique and for the memory of a major personality. There are, in addition, other points to be considered. The first can be summed up by the use of the single word *attack,* since that is the very first thing that strikes the spectator even if the attack be faulty or vulgar. By *attack* I mean the intensity of the performer, her degree of concentration and especially her sense of climax. I mean negatively her lack of an apologetic attitude. That last is at present the failing of the average British dancer. She is so technically conscientious that one can notice the exact moment at which her physical powers are beginning to be strained. She goes on trying valiantly with an apologetic attitude for any shortcomings and it is on this note that she ends her variation. The performer with real attack knows how to reserve herself for a climax, she is conscious of this and does not feel the need for apology. She has a feeling of superiority over her audience. In that sense she is not the servant of her public.

I will not carry comparisons between British and foreign dancers any further. There is more nonsense talked on this subject than any other. There will always be snobs whom no amount of evidence will convince and who enjoy the luxury of the imported article only because it is imported. We must guard against injustice to our own and also against chauvinism or complacency. Recent attacks on our ballet in a book purporting to give an account of a distinguished foreign company can be ignored. They bear not the slightest relationship to the facts. Fonteyn, May, Shearer, Gray, Brae, and Helpmann and the others supply a crushing answer.

The next point to be considered, and it is related to the first, is continuity of movement. Every dance, at any rate in the classical and romantic ballets, is made up of a series of classroom steps. Words have to be made into phrases and the phrases must add up to a poem. We must forget the " cat," " mat," " dog," " door," " father," " mother " of the schoolroom. The dance must be conceived as a whole, must be as fluid as the music. *The solo dancer, if photographed in a whole dance on one enormous plate, must make a harmonious dancing frieze.* That is the essence of great dancing. It rules out those hard, forceful and dazzling performances that are sometimes mistakenly called classical. Such classicism is spurious and will only deceive the tyro. There are never many dancers at any one period who entirely fulfil this last condition. We call it poetry or fluidity but it is something that could be proved by the use of an ultra rapid camera.

Finally two other factors must be carefully considered before any comparisons with the past are of value. Our dancers to-day are younger and much harder worked and their repertoire is a very much larger one. They must shine in *Swan*

Lake and *Miracle in the Gorbals, Les Sylphides* and *Adam Zero*. Ninette de Valois, as great an analyst as she is a creative artist and an administrator, has, in a lecture, called this a " diffusion " of technique, an excellent phrase so long as it is not carried too far or used as an excuse for faulty work. The contemporary dancer is in no sense a utility dancer and I have not the slightest patience with those who invoke the past to damn the present. At that rate Legnani would have prevented the emergence of Kchesinska and the Russian school and the Russians in their turn would have blocked the progress of our young English dancers.

2.—TYPES OF DANCER

We must next remember that there are certain very definite types of dancer and if we attempt to fit a dancer into the wrong type and criticise her accordingly everything that we say will be completely erroneous and unjust. Certain dancers of real quality refuse to be labelled in any convenient museum fashion. We shall see at least one such dancer in our gallery of portraits.

Much confusion arises from the wrong use in this country and in America of the word *ballerina* as a synonym for dancer. Ballerina is a title denoting rank which in a state ballet is as official as the rank of general, though a good deal scarcer, while in a non-state ballet it signifies the leading dancer who is entrusted with the great classic rôles. But quite apart from being a rank it signifies a definite type of dancer, and here we are concerned with types. The ballerina requires a special physique. She must not be taller than five feet six inches, since she will be doing so much work with a partner, she must have well shaped legs, since her traditional uniform is the revealing *tutu,* she must be reasonably good looking, she always impersonates an enchanted princess, her points — that is the tip of her toes — must be a strong platform on which to support the weight of her body. She must be well turned out from the hips, free from all strain. She requires perfect poise, mental and physical, a dominating personality and that sense of attack highly developed. With all these gifts she may yet be a failure, lacking a musical sense or the power to co-ordinate. Granted that she has every attribute, then she is fully qualified to dance the great classical rôles which were specially designed to be interpreted by just such a dancer. Probably also she will be versatile with a wide range, as was Karsavina, and as are Fonteyn, Chauviré, Danilova, Baronova and Toumanova. A Trefilova, supreme classical ballerina, was an exception, limited more by temperament than anything else to the diamond-hard brilliance of the classics.

Then there is the near-ballerina, an unofficial but a very real classification. That is the dancer who can on occasion dance the ballerina rôles with charm, but who excels in the more dreamy and romantic rôles such as in *Les Sylphides,* where arms are softer and there is no need to dominate the whole stage. The

8

true ballerina is a rarity, there are but a handful in a generation. The near-ballerina is far more frequent; she is the utility dancer of to-day.

The next division is the demi-caractère dancer often included in the near-ballerina class. She is the *soubrette,* with a romantic or sentimental rôle to act. The ballerina is *the dancer* whatever her rôle, demi-caractère shows us the dancer *as* Columbine or *as* a serving maid. Finally there is the character dancer who does not exploit the finer points of the orthodox technique but who acts a " heavy " rôle or who performs the national dances of some particular country.

It is absurd to say categorically that the ballerina is the best dancer and to leave it at that. It depends on the particular ballerina. A Karsavina was a great ballerina. She was equally great in demi-caractère or in pure character. She could dance *Swan Lake, Carnaval* and *Le Tricorne* with equal perfection. Our own Fonteyn is equally at home in *Swan Lake, Carnaval* or the barefoot dancing of *Dante Sonata.* On the other hand a Riabouchinska was completely inadequate in the one performance she danced of *Swan Lake,* but judging her in the prelude of *Les Sylphides* or in the many rôles she made so absolutely her own I would rank her well above her contemporary Russian ballerinas both as a dancer and an artist.

It is always difficult to judge a dancer purely through seeing her in a rôle she has created in a modern ballet. There is the case of Nina Verchinina, superb in *Les Présages* and *Choreartium,* in which she made an unforgettable impression. Was she a great dancer or did Massine create these rôles round her personality and physique? That from the critic's point of view is the great value of the classical and neo-romantic ballets. They are his yardstick. A Rose Adagio, a Blue Bird, a Prelude from *Les Sylphides, Swan Lake* Adagio, *Giselle* Acts 1 and 2, Swanhilda in *Coppelia,* immediately tell us everything about the dancer we are watching. They even reveal character to a degree that is astonishing to the amateur.

3.—THE MALE DANCER

So far I have spoken of the dancer in the feminine, but the same points of criticism arise with the male dancer. A particular quality required by the male dancer, apart from the essential virility so often lacking, is chivalry or nobility. It is his task to be self-effacing at the right moment and to centre the attention of the audience on his partner. A true *danseur noble* can double the effect of a ballerina's work.

To-day we in England as opposed to France and the Slavonic countries are sadly lacking in male dancers. The intake of men into the schools, though growing, is still very small. Also the younger age at which dancers now appear affects the male adversely, since virility is an essential requisite. The continued call up of men to the Forces is a handicap that cannot be overcome.

The important dancers of our period are not the classical ones nor the great technicians, understood in the narrow sense, but the actor-choreographers, Massine and Helpmann, who have brought something new to ballet, something that they have had the physical urge to express in themselves in the first place.

4.—THE INFLUENCE OF DANCERS ON BALLET

The dancer is naturally the most publicised person in the ballet team. Most people imagine that she is the whole ballet, even though the vast majority to-day realise that she does not improvise the movements from performance to performance. There are a few who see her as a beautiful puppet dangled by a choreographer who must bear a strong resemblance to the astrologer in *Petrouchka*.

Both of these views are wide of the mark but it is very important in such a study to see where the truth lies.

Given a school of standing and authority with all the resources of a state behind it, then the supply of dancers of technical efficiency is adequate. Among their numbers there will be a small percentage above the average. This means that the choreographer can fulfil his intentions and find the cast that fits into his scheme. Under such circumstances the influence of the individual dancer on ballet in general should not be too direct. She is still far from being a marionette and her personality plays its part in the interpretation of the rôle but it does not bend or distort it or force the choreographer to modify his original intention. That is the general rule, but ballet is not based on a factory conveyor-belt system. It is concerned with the inter-play of strong and conflicting personalities. Individual dancers because of their particular physique or temperament have powerfully affected the history of the dance.

This is not the place to delve into history but certain examples must be quoted. Taglioni was the embodiment of romanticism, the very dancer to bring the wilis and sylphs to life on the stage. Though the romantic movement, for reasons right outside ballet, was in full swing in all the arts and would in any case have found its way into ballet, it was Taglioni who gave it the Sylphide direction. Her popularity was similar to that of Pavlova 75 years after, and though she had rivals she was *the* dancer. " Will the young folk ever see anything so charming, anything so classic, anything like Taglioni? " wrote Thackeray in *Pendennis*. It was Taglioni who first gave us the conception of the dancer as a bird-spirit just alighting or about to take off, and who consequently stressed the rôle of the points, tips of the toes, so much abused later when the original conception was forgotten.

Virginia Zucchi, an Italian dancer, who appeared in St Petersburg, danced in the most tawdry and artificial ballets that would seem like burlesque at the present day. They did then to such sensitive people as Alexandre Benois and his circle. But Zucchi was an extraordinary artist, sensitive, poetical and a magnificent actress. Through rising superior to her material she drew the attention of Benois, and through him, Diaghileff, to the possibilities of ballet as an artistic medium. She also inspired the young Russian dancers. There can be no doubt at all that she exercised a powerful revivifying effect on ballet.

Pavlova, like Taglioni, inspired a new romantic wave, but before her influence could be complete she left Russian Ballet to head a company of her own. Her influence was still great but in the inspiration she gave to the dancers of the future and not on choreography.

The influence of the dancer is greatest in a commercial concern where there is no school to draw upon and where the choreographer must use the dancers available. The de Basil Ballet with its choreographers Balanchine and later Massine was more directly influenced and controlled by dancers than any other organisation of equal standing. Toumanova and Baronova had learnt through their great teacher Preobrajenska how to perform multiple turns in a manner that made the thirty-two fouettés from *Swan Lake* into a commonplace. These turns were used with startling dramatic effect in *Cotillon*, *Concurrence* and *Jeux D'Enfants*. The unformed personalities of the brilliant child dancers were also effectively used, especially by Balanchine. When they grew up some of the effects were lost. Nina Verchinina's special plastic gifts so dramatically revealed in *Les Présages* were repeated in *Choreartium*. In her absence these symphonic works greatly suffered. It was this undoubted dancer-domination that first revived interest in ballet, especially through the Baronova-Toumanova rivalry but that later disrupted that magnificent company.

Fokine's ideal was a strong company in which he could find dancers for every conception. He did not believe that the choreographer should seek inspiration in the individual. He wanted the strong dancer free of all mannerisms. This was no denial of personality. Fokine had no use for a machine. " The greatness of Karsavina," he once told me, " was that she could fit into and then embellish every creation. I did not have to think: can she do this or that? "

5.—A SENSE OF PROPORTION

There can be no doubt that dancer-domination disrupts a company. If Mlle. X is the one person who can make a real success of a certain rôle, she has the management in the hollow of her hand and would be a saint not to take some advantage of it. There is a disastrous system used in America by which the impresario, up to a point an astute business man, has by contract a say in the casting of rôles in the large cities. Apart from the fact that he is not in a position to decide and that his action brings the management into contempt with its artistes this means that there can be no variation of cast and that the young unknown has no chance in front of a critical audience. The impresario chooses certain dancers as stars, turns his magnificent publicity machine on to them and persuades the public that if they do not appear the public is not getting its moneysworth. This use or rather abuse of dancers will kill ballet more surely and more rapidly than anything I know. By all means let a manager protect himself by a clause in the contract stipulating for the appearance during the season of some six out of ten names, but the casting concerns the director alone. The splendid company that we knew as Colonel de Basil's Monte Carlo Ballet has provided the nucleus for a number of troupes built around his original dancers, who have thereby assumed an altogether ridiculous importance.

Let us realise that the company is more important than the individual and that it has a personality of its own. Nijinsky, " star of stars," leaves Diaghileff, but Diaghileff continues. The Diaghileff Ballet had its founder's powerful personality as its major asset. It should never be forgotten that the ballet we know to-day is a repertory company and not a star-ridden Broadway venture. It is impossible for the ballerina to take her spell in the *corps de ballet* for a number of obvious reasons, not the least of which is physical, but in the repertory company there is a sense of equality and a realisation that each one contributes to a whole. Once the dancers realise that fact a company becomes a happy one, providing the right atmosphere for creative work. I have heard—this began after de Basil's annual visits to America — dancers quoted like stocks and shares. The lack of stability that resulted has gone far to kill *Ballet Russe,* as distinct from Russian Ballet. And with the many new companies arising it is necessary to create new stars in a hurry until the balletic solar system is ablaze—with shooting stars not planets.

Our own system is less spectacular, an adaptation of state methods: from School to Sadlers Wells, from Sadlers Wells to Covent Garden. We have our ballerina and many first rate artists who need experience and are getting it, because casting is done by experienced and responsible persons and does not depend upon the caprice of a business man. Every one of our young dancers could be boosted artificially into a star and dubbed " ballerina " by a busy publicity department aided by a team of photographers. I have watched this process many times. It has never yet made for artistic success, personal happiness, or even good business. A Ballet Company is a team in which dancers take their places with stage staff, musicians, designers, choreographers and management.

I would add one more unit to the team, my readers, the general public. By their attitude they can enormously help or hinder the artistic growth of dancers. In the long run they are largely responsible for the type of dancing they see.

CHAPTER II — PAVLOVA AND KARSAVINA

A STUDY IN DANCING TYPES

In the previous chapter I wrote of certain dancers who had set a standard of performance. I also warned my readers against the negative pastime of looking for second Pavlovas or Karsavinas. I have, however, chosen those two dancers for discussion, not only because of the great position they occupy in the history of our art or because of the richness of the memories their work has left behind, but also because they represent two distinct types, types that tend to be repeated, though the individual artists are, of course, unique.

Pavlova moved exquisitely, at times, even when only taking a call, more exquisitely than I have ever seen anyone move. She reacted emotionally to music and was able to convey that emotion powerfully to her audience. Her technique was limited, but only in extent never in quality. Her dramatic range was as limited in some respects as that of the Victorian keepsake painter, taking in the field between the romantic grief of *Giselle* and the charming mischief of *La Fille Mal Gardée*. She could make a trifle into something memorable that made one forgive the prettiness of her costume and the often mediocre music that descended to the inanities of a Pugni or a Minkus. Nobody else could have done that. She was essentially an individualist around whom the whole performance had to centre, a dancer with a spotlight eternally trained on her. She might have influenced the entire choreography of her time. She did not. Her appeal was not to the small group of artists who swayed opinion but to every man and his wife, in whom she planted a firm if unreasoning love of the dance.

All of these things make one ask the questions: Was Pavlova a great ballerina? Was Pavlova a great artist?

The answer to the first question must largely rest on her performance of *Giselle,* the only true test that she allowed herself in Western Europe, and in *Giselle* she was unsurpassed among those whom I have seen. She was thoroughly in tune with its romanticism, and even its music must have found an emotional reaction in her. I cannot picture her, for instance, in the technical *Casse Noisette* or in Act II. of *Swan Lake*. She had none of the diamond hardness of a Trefilova. Taglioni-like she excelled in impersonations of the ephemeral, a flower, a dragonfly, the dying swan. She does not fit into one's picture of the classical ballerina of her time, but is rather a throwback to the romanticism of the 1830's.

The second question is more difficult to answer and depends very much upon one's definition of " great artist " and upon the degree of conscious artistry that the critic demands. From some points of view it takes a very great artist to make the trivial into a moving experience, to make the *Fairy Doll,* for instance, not only tolerable but a real delight. How she lit up the stage when she came down the stairs, making one forget the horribly dated music, the obvious choreography and the tinsel setting! I doubt, however, whether she was a conscious artist. I believe that there was in her something of the medium who felt and then conveyed powerful emotions that were neither reasoned not selective. She was certainly devoid of real taste or discrimination. Benois summed her up admirably when he said that she performed theatrical miracles by making the tawdry and commonplace memorable.

There is a whole class of dancers of the Pavlova type, though lacking her enormous magnetism. They move gracefully because they cannot help it, they feel music without really understanding it, they share their emotions to the full. I do not wish to underrate Pavlova. I would give much to see her once again if only for an instant or two in one of those small divertissements such as *Californian Poppy,* in which the folding of her petals was so infinitely moving, a true drama where the tawdry effects of a *Don Quixote* or an *Amaryllis* saddened one by the waste of effort. Neither do I wish to underrate those instinctive dancers whose movements are a joy to watch and who, when rightly cast, are so much nearer to great theatrical art than those who reason but do so faultily.

Tamara Karsavina stands at the very opposite extreme. Her range was enormous. She was a member of what was the most remarkable team of artists the ballet has seen. She profoundly influenced the ballet of her period. Her dancing leaves not only a memory but a model. Apart from her individual brilliance she is the true product of a fine education that could only be reproduced under ideal circumstances.

Consider for a moment the various rôles with which she is associated, not forgetting the classics that she danced in her native Russia. There was the neo-romanticism of *Les Sylphides* and *Le Spectre de La Rose.* This second ballet in which she was unsurpassed I must have watched innumerable times both from the auditorium and the wings. It was a perfectly controlled, perfectly reasoned performance in which every gesture had been carefully studied. Karsavina was not carried away by the music, she understood it perfectly and set out to interpret it. Yet this deliberation was never for a moment evident. The effect that one received nightly was that this drama of adolescence was happening for the first time. From this touching white-romanticism she plunged straight into the exotic and highly coloured romanticism of a *Cleopatra, Schéhérazade* and *Thamar;* a jump quite beyond the instinctive art. In *Thamar* she interpreted music that was balletically difficult, since it lacked the immediate narrative force of *Schéhérazade* and brought to life Lermontov's heroine, making herself a part of Bakst's decorative scheme. That is of the essence of Karsavina's art, the ability to belong to a whole, to form part of a picture without a loss of personality. Karsavina's personality was perfectly controlled. One did not say immediately, " that is Karsavina," but " that is Thamar, or Columbine or the Dancer in *Petrouchka*. Then as a complete contrast and later in her career we see her as the Miller's Wife in *Le Chapeau Tricorne*. I do not speak of the new dance idiom, we expect that in a highly trained dancer, but the entirely fresh creation of character, of Karsavina as an integral part of the Massine-Picasso-de Falla conception. It has been danced by many, sometimes brilliantly, but always as a *tour de force*. With Karsavina nothing was a *tour de force*. Once her reason had shown her the way everything appeared perfectly natural. Pavlova as Spaniard or Gypsy was always the great Russian dancer in an exotic costume. It is true that " St Petersburg Spanish " was the idiom of her youth and training, but the point is that she must have liked it since she chose it deliberately.

We have caught a glimpse of Karsavina's mind at work in her remarkable autobiography, *Theatre Street*. No young dancer and no ballet enthusiast can afford to miss this classic. It shows the background required by a dancer, if she is to be a conscious artist, truly equipped to belong to a creative organisation.

Just as with Pavlova, the opposite extreme, there is a Karsavina type, the dancer who reasons. And that is the type of dancer that present day ballet with its enormous and constantly expanding dramatic range requires.

The example is there, but the machinery is still faulty. If only the dancers and their teachers realise what it meant to dance like Karsavina, half the battle will have been won. " You can only express yourself," she said, " when technique has become second nature." To-day in the majority of dancing schools there is too much preoccupation with steps and not enough with the dance and what it can express. Steps are for the class and not for the stage. They are certainly not for the audience whose concern must be with the finished product. Never was a little knowledge so dangerous. The counting of *fouettés* means the death of ballet as an expressive art.

An age that has produced a Pavlova and a Karsavina is indeed a rich one that can rival those of Camargo and Sallé, Taglioni and Elssler. A Pavlova is a " sport," a Karsavina points the way to the future. She is essentially the perfect modern dancer.

15

Isadora Duncan was strongly opposed throughout her whole life to the art of ballet. She found it stilted and artificial. While she admired Pavlova as a dancer she deeply regretted what she considered the technical limitations of Pavlova's art. Yet Duncan's influence on the art form that she depised was a great one. while her influence on the dance outside ballet has been negligible. In any study of dancers it is essential to include Duncan since her name is so often invoked to prove a number of contradictory points. First let us be quite clear about Duncan herself. She was a very great artist, a very great dancer, and creative to a high degree.

This means that it is possible to become a great dancer without having had a single lesson in an orthodox technique. Duncan was inspired; a thoroughly unsatisfactory explanation except to those who watched her dance. We can dismiss all that she herself has written on the sources of her inspiration or on her technique all that her followers have written. They are merely attempts to rationalise this inspiration . To understand her it is necessary not to read but to look at the works of Rodin, de Segonzac, Maurice Denis, Bourdelle, and others, or to study exactly what it was that she gave to ballet.

Duncan was inspired, her art was strictly personal and so was her technique. It was a technique developed to suit her particular physique and temperament; her's and no one else's. It was for all that a very real technique, though she varied more from performance to performance than any ballet-trained dancer.

Duncan flourished at a time when the dancer was fettered in every direction: through cumbersome conventional costume, through inane music, through massive and gaudy scenic settings, through the abuse of a technique that had become master instead of slave.

She freed the body from corset and *tutu*. Sallé had attempted it in *Pygmalion* in the early eighteenth century and had failed. She freed the dancer from the puerilities of Minkus and Pugni. Ballet, too, had started with Lully and Rameau, but with the exception of Tchaikovsky was no longer true to itself. She freed the stage from M.-G.-M. ' musical ' scenery *avant l'heure,* and showed the beauty of simple drapes. She stressed the fact that technique is a means and not an end, and this at a time when the public was raving about 32 *fouettés* and believing them to be a genuine dancing accomplishment.

What a programme. What a revolt. Yet she was re-stating something that ballet itself had known and forgotten.

TAMARA TOUMANOVA

NORA KAYE

Duncan came to St Petersburg at the end of Petipa's reign and before Fokine had been given his opportunity to save ballet. Her exact influence on his work must remain a moot point. Diaghileff states it to have been very great indeed. Certainly Fokine was already working in the same direction. Putting her influence at its lowest, her example enormously facilitated his task, inspiring Diaghileff himself with confidence.

Every " free dancer " may imagine herself a Duncan, every girl who has ever been photographed in draperies with a Parthenon background takes her name in vain. It is in ballet that we can see her to-day, and if ballet forgets Duncan and what she stood for, it will rapidly degenerate.

I repeat once more that it is possible to be a great dancer outside the orthodox technique, but this is as rare as to make art of such a sugary trifle as *Christmas*. Both may be classed as " theatrical miracles."

CHAPTER IV —ALICIA MARKOVA

ANGLO-RUSSIAN DANCER

Until comparatively recently it was essential for a dancer to have a foreign name, preferably a Russian one, and since English dancers formed a part of either the Pavlova or the Diaghileff Company this was a perfectly logical thing. Their training was often Russian and certainly their artistic surroundings, from the moment that they joined the ballet, were purely Russian. Whatever may be said about the public reaction to such names, the dancers can scarcely be accused of snobbery.

When Diaghileff was cut off by War and Revolution from his natural supply of dancers in Russia, he found a substitute in the English dancer whose abilities he greatly admired. There had been one great English dancer in his Company from the very earliest days to the end. Lydia Sokolova cannot be thought of as an Anglo-Russian, so completely did she assimilate herself into the Company. But the others may be termed Anglo-Russian dancers, and they numbered among them such fine performers as Ninette de Valois, Vera Savina, Anton Dolin and Alicia Markova. Their technical equipment was well in advance of Diaghileff's other newscomers. Ninette de Valois was the only dancer he had at one period capable of performing a rapid classical variation. Her " finger " variation and the Blue Bird of Savina and Dolin still linger in the memory. Markova and Dolin played a major rôle in the waiting period between the death of Diaghileff and the establishment of our own ballet. They had a name and a rich experience upon which to draw. Sometimes they seemed a little ill at ease in the strange environment of an English Company, and the beginnings of our choreography may well have seemed a little childish to them after the sophisticated modernism of Diaghileff's final phase. Our ballet, especially in Camargo days, was a somewhat slipshod affair, far removed from the disciplined touch of that master stage director, Serge Grigorieff. This was the beginning of Markova's second career.

Alicia Markova was a pupil of that fine teacher and lovable eccentric, the late Seraphine Astafieva. After a very short time she showed an altogether exceptional promise, both helped and handicapped by a superficial physical resemblance to Pavlova. It speaks wonders for her that she has managed to live it down. The description " miniature Pavlova " so infuriated the worthy Astafieva when she first saw the child that she nearly refused to teach her. Only Markova's simplicity and obvious talent made her overcome the prejudice. Markova joined the Diaghileff Ballet at the age of fourteen, and, let it be remembered, that at that time baby ballerinas were completely unknown and the idea was not looked upon with much favour. She was too small and distinctive to take her place in the Corps de Ballet, and Diaghileff nursed her carefully, giving her strengthening lessons with the great *maestro* Cecchetti. Her first rôle was in a small excerpt from *Swan Lake,* and there is no doubt, after the success that she made in it, that she would have been promoted to ballerina in the later Russian Ballet, but Diaghileff was too wise for that. She owes her subsequent great career to his wisdom. She next appeared as Little Red Riding Hood in *Aurora's Wedding* and as the mischievous child in *La Boutique Fantasque,* small rôles in which she was seen to advantage. Her first creation was the Nightingale in Balanchine's ballet of that name. The work itself was a failure, but it had taught Markova how to handle a sustained rôle. Her first big hit was in Balanchine's *La Chatte,* where she alternated with Nikitina in the title rôle. She more than held her own, proving herself a magnificent instrument in the choreographer's hands.

At the death of Diaghileff, Markova had a reputation of promise and nothing more. She was almost unknown outside the small circle of balletomanes. She fulfilled a number of commercial engagements that called for mechanical brilliance and she revealed that she possessed that brilliance and the ability to hold the stage. But it was with the birth of our British ballet that she came into her own, dancing for the Camargo Society, Marie Rambert's Ballet Club and Sadlers Wells. At Sadlers Wells she became the bright particular star with the little company as a background. For her, they revived the great classics in their entirety, and she filled the theatre in *Swan Lake, Casse Noisette* and *Giselle.* The second act of her *Giselle* made an altogether extraordinary impression; rarely had we seen a dancer touch the ground so lightly. The first act was less moving and more stylised. There is, however, plenty of justification in a work that is classical in style though romantic in feeling, especially when the music gives so little true romantic incentive. It was Markova who revealed the full beauties of classicism that had been dormant for so very long, and won a new public to ballet. It was, however, in the small intimate Mercury Theatre of Marie Rambert's Ballet Club that she learned to create new rôles. There can be no doubt that her co-operation helped to develop the young Frederick Ashton, to-day in his full power as Britain's leading choreographer. Ashton also helped to discover Markova, studying her carefully as he created for her such rôles as *La Péri.* But Markova has essentially the aloof temperament of the classical ballerina and is only seen at her very best in a rôle that does not require very great emotional qualities or the portrayal of some positive character. Although so often compared to Pavlova, no two dancers could be more different, either in temperament or technique. Markova has an unbelievable lightness but lacks the joy or the warmth that could make Pavlova shine in the most trivial divertissement.

CHAPTER V. — PEARL ARGYLE: A GREAT PIONEER

Pearl Argyle must occupy an important position in any dance history of the early 'thirties, a position out of all proportion to her actual technical abilities. It was not only her great physical beauty—and of all the dancers she was the most beautiful—but her very real artistry that first drew critical attention to the possibilities of the English dancer. Markova was an Anglo-Russian, an inheritor of the great tradition, but Pearl Argyle was English, and the English dancer had been denied by most of the English public the slightest personality. She was popularly supposed to be a rather dry but well disciplined automaton. Pearl Argyle broke down this superstition, attracting not only an English audience but the attention of both Balanchine and Massine.

As a pupil of Marie Rambert, she first shone at the Ballet Club, both in excerpts from the classics and in creations by Frederick Ashton, Andrée Howard and Antony Tudor. She had started ballet comparatively late, her technique was never strong, but her artistry was so mature compared to the more technical dancers that her technical shortcomings were hidden. There was about her work an extraordinary serenity. Her ability as an actress was limited, but in the right rôle she made an unforgettable impression. Two such rôles were created for her by Ashton, Venus in *Mars and Venus,* where she interpreted Scarlatti to perfection, and as *The Lady of Shallot,* in a Tennysonian pre-Raphaelite ballet of that name, a little gem of *ballet intime.* In that the serene Pearl Argyle showed true temperament and was particularly moving, since she held so much in reserve. In the Camargo and early Sadlers Wells days Pearl Argyle's work was especially important. She was surrounded by young dancers who were technically her superiors, but who had as yet little stagecraft or maturity of expression. She filled the stage. She had, for instance, in *Swan Lake,* the presence, the walk of the ballerina, and her style convinced even though the brilliance was lacking.

Among my most treasured memories is her performance in the *Gods Go 4'begging.* It was perfection. Of her it could be truly written that " a smile hovered about her lips like a bird flutters about a rose."

She was, I feel, wise to retire when she did. The Wells youngsters were rapidly developing artistically and their superior technique would have limited Pearl Argyle more and more in the rôles that she could have taken. She was a pioneer and none of the audiences of that time will forget either her beauty or the use that she made of it.

[Since writing this chapter I have learnt of the tragic death of Pearl Argyle.
I have left it unaltered.—A.L.H.]

CHAPTER VI. — RIABOUCHINSKA

A PORTRAIT FROM MEMORY
(*Written in a nostalgic mood from a Warden's Post, 1943*)

1.—THE VINTAGE OF 1932

The year 1932-3 was a revolutionary one from the point of view of dancing. With the death of Diaghileff, we had seen the end of " dancing in the grand manner." Indeed it died a little before the end of his reign, leaving one magnificent survivor, Alexandra Danilova, who was to make a second and greater career in the new phase.

Diaghileff's restricted type of repertoire after his failure with *The Sleeping Princess* in 1921 did not call for great classical virtuosity and painters and composers stole most of the limelight, badly upsetting the balance. Angular and jerky movements were a negation of Russian classicism and at times the dancers might have been replaced by marionettes with little loss to the whole. Technically the most accomplished young dancers were the English recruits, de Valois, Savina, Markova, then just beginning to show promise, and Dolin. I speak of the recruits, there were still strong dancers of the old regime: Tchernicheva, Sokolova, the inimitable Lopokova, Idzikovski and Leon Woizikovski.

While Diaghileff was presenting his last creations the new generation of dancers were in school in Paris, where the great Russian dancers of a pre-Diaghileff tradition had opened studios. There was Olga Preobrajenska, who had triumphed over a mediocre physique by will power, intelligence and hard work. She had a highly analytical mind and was always interested in cause and effect. She had mastered in particular the difficulties, physical and mental, of those multiple turns that made so effective if also so acrobatic a climax to a variation. She excelled especially in the grounding of children.

There was Matilde Kchesinska, dazzling and undisputed *prima ballerina assoluta* of the Maryinsky, highly intelligent and a remarkable mistress of polish, showmanship and dramatic climax.

There was Lubov Egorova, who specialised in the master class in which the finished artist could gain speed, confidence and a knowledge of the great rôles.

In addition there were Alexandre Volinine and Vera Trefilova.

Girls from all over the world found their way to these Paris studios, but the outstanding pupils were members of the Russian emigration.

These new young dancers gave something fresh to ballet. They were brought up in an atmosphere of classicism, sometimes even a *démodé* classicism, far from the angular acrobatics of Diaghileff's final phase. They revealed to the public not only their fresh young personalities but all the beauties of a virtuosity

23

hidden since 1921. For a time they restored the balance by bringing the dancer back to her rightful position and then they disrupted it again in the opposite direction. Theirs was not the true " grand manner," their education had been too hurried for that. They excelled in the more sensational feats but often failed in the groundwork. They had after all crammed into three or four years what it takes nine or ten to learn. Also they had had few opportunities of watching great dancers in great works.

The impact of their performances was tremendous. It not only restored ballet to favour, it enormously extended its public and scope. Had they been given the necessary quiet and stability they might have gone a great deal furth.r. America had a fatal effect. Imagine what happens to a dancer who appears in 103 towns in seven months. Is it to be wondered at if she looks longingly at Hollywood or Broadway with a return to ballet as a guest artist?

I include a full length portrait from memory of, perhaps, the most unusual and interesting of these nursery products of the vintage years 1932-33. It can stand as a prototype.

2.—THE ARTIST

Looking back, not centuries as it now seems, but only ten years ago, to the first appearance of the De Basil babies, those fledgling ballerinas that took London by storm, it is always the image of Riabouchinska that predominates. Not the memory of some faultless technical performance or of some dazzling feat of virtuosity, but of a complete and consistent artistic personality who made her rôles her own in a manner not one of the newcomers had done; not necessarily a measure of greatness in dancing, but greatness in dancing alone has long ceased to be of major interest.

In 1933, when we first had an opportunity of seeing her—her visit as a child with the *Chauve Souris* does not count—she was overshadowed by Toumanova, a magnificent dancer of outstanding beauty, who had been carefully measured by Balanchine for her rôles in *Mozartiana, Songes, Cotillon* and *Concurrence,* and by Baronova, who not only had the technical equipment and poise of a miniature ballerina, but a dramatic range from the light comedy of the Midinette of *Le Beau Danube* to the mature passion of *Les Présages.*

In that first season we saw Riabouchinska in a variety of rôles, *Les Préages, Cotillon, Jeux d'Enfants, Le Beau Danube, Scuola di Ballo.* Dramatically these had one thing in common; they were light, airy and gay.

In *Scuola di Ballo* and *Le Beau Danube* the rôles were those of the conventional demi-caractère soubrette, well within the grasp of any competent dancer of taste, and it was only possible to gauge Riabouchinska's unusual personality and artistry when the competent dancer of taste replaced her. The rôles still existed,

24

at times their dancers distinguished themselves, but something positive was missing. The feeling of spontaneity that Riabouchinska had; a lightness of mind equal to her lightness of dancing. The understudy acted, Riabouchinska lived, a distinction that is not convincing in words but that was very real in fact, as one realised when one saw the complete repertoire without her.

In *Cotillon* she supplied the gaiety that was an essential contrast to the mystical core, of that magnificent choreographic poem. The accent was on the dark Toumanova, the fair Riabouchinska pointed that contrast and was content to leave the rôle as a supporting one, never stealing the limelight as the brilliant costume and the dancing involved gave her the opportunity of doing; a sense of dramatic measure rare in a child. We shall have an opportunity of seeing that Riabouchinska along among the younger dancers has never over-acted.

Frivolity in *Les Présages* had no set rôle from a narrative point of view; there was nothing to develop, just a musical mood to interpret. A light contrast to the passion and heroism of the other scenes, but only Riabouchinska could sustain this seemingly easy rôle, that is " easy " to the modern technical product of the Paris studios. Without her it was a blank or worse, a mere exhibition of fireworks that the wedding cake costume rendered intolerably banal. What exactly she gave to the rôle it is difficult to say. Perhaps that gaiety of spirit that is the stamp of the great artist, something quite apart from the spirited interpretation of a humorous rôle. Dramatic mime can be comparatively simple to put across the footlights, gaiety never. In discussing Pavlova with me once, Fokine picked on *Christmas* or the simple Fan Dance as the true test of Pavlova's greatness. " Imagine them danced by anyone else," he said.

It was in the surrealist, *Jeux d'Enfants,* that one could grasp more positively during that first season the unusual quality of this artist. The rôle was a complex one, the impression of a gawky child who must show when she falls in love with one of the creatures of her imagining that the girl is mother of the woman. The sentimental could have no place at all here. The rôle asked for nothing more than the faintest suggestion of childishness, it was never a child's study as in *La Boutique Fantasque.* It called for the hint that these fantastic dream happenings arose in the mind of this strange Paris-studio-Alice.

Riabouchinska was masterly in her handling of this, and her interpretation improved in the six years I watched her dance it. If it started as unconscious artistry, it became fully conscious as she developed. That gives us a clue to Riabouchinska's success. In the case of her contemporaries the reverse was often the case. Toumanova in *Cotillon* and Boronova in *Le Beau Danube* soon lost some of the freshness of the first season's performances. They had grown out of those particular rôles. Another way of saying that they could not rationalise and copy what had been instinctive originally and what ingenious choreographers had built around their immature personalities.

The critic writing after one performance or even summing up the work of a whole season cannot properly assess an immature artist. He can only talk of her work as it strikes him at the time. If he expresses himself at all positively, as he must if he is to give more than a wishy-washy commentary, he runs the risk of being accused of inconsistency, but in fact he does not change his standards—it is the young dancer who changes, not only in quality but also in physique and execution. The only alternative is for him to tie a permanent label to each dancer, the most appropriate variation of the words dainty or vivacious. In 1933, Riabouchinska was only potentially outstanding, her personality was strangely elusive, but when I last saw her in 1939 she was in a class of her own.

Riabouchinska, like Pavlova, has always been a difficult artist to discuss. She created a new word, her own name to describe her rôle in dancing. That is true, though of course to a far lesser degree, of Riabouchinska. There is a certain affinity between Riabouchinska and Pavlova, a quality that no less a judge than the late Victor Dandré, Pavlova's husband, himself noticed, with all the reservations that anyone of sense must make in using the great ballerina's name. In *Paganini,* for instance, one of the most lyrical interpretations ever given by Riabouchinska, that affinity was very evident. I rank her performance in that ballet, which as a whole I find indifferent, among the most moving I have seen on the ballet stage.

So far I have only discussed creations, but the same is the case with two other Fokine roles of the grand period, the Prelude in *Les Sylphides* and *Le Spectre de la Rose.*

The *Sylphides* Prelude is to my mind, from an interpretative point of view, the infallible test of artistry in a romantic type of dancer. A touch can make it sentimental, too much dreaminess dull, hard arms trivial, and there is no virtuosity to hide the expression of the face. The focal point here is the dancer's face. The same applies to *Le Spectre de la Rose,* but in this I have never seen Riabouchinska with a partner who could make the whole thing live, and her performance is but a fragment. What was interesting was the fact that it did not in any way follow the lines of Karsavina, but was a thing all on its own.

Her very popular performance of the Blue Bird in *Aurora's Wedding* is not, classically speaking, an outstanding one. She has no bravura in her make up. It is attractive, because she herself is attractive, but it is not the Petipa Blue Bird that she shows us, but a Blue Bird that has fluttered around Fokine's enchanted garden, that has the mistiness of a Corot and not the precision of an Ingres. Riabouchinska is not a ballerina at all. She is one of those dancers who refuse to be classified. I saw her solitary performance of *Swan Lake.* It was a dismal failure. I believe, however, that her Giselle would in parts be dramatically memorable, even if it lacked the essential classical precision. Riabouchinska is not naturally musical in the same manner as Toumanova, Baronova, and especially that most musical of dancers, Fonteyn. She must and she does study her rôles

MARKOVA

LEONIDE MASSINE

ROBERT HELPMANN

IRENE SKORIK

NINA VERCHININA

with painstaking care, never relying on brilliant improvisation. She builds them up, inviting criticism as she proceeds, and she herself possesses a highly developed critical faculty.

To complete this portrait, it is necessary to visit Riabouchinska behind the scenes.

It is, I know, from long experience, not only possible but easy to deduce a dancer's character from her performances, especially after watching her in a sequence of classical rôles that have no positive dramatic content but that rely solely on the dancer for interpretation. That is one of the innumerable enjoyments of watching dancing. Strictly speaking, it may lie outside the critic's province; at times it would surely expose him to libel suits, but to give as complete a picture as possible of one of those young dancers who have revived and popularised an old art is well worth attempting without the necessity of inserting anecdotes of the Hollywood star type which are of course as studio-manufactured as their films. Contemporary portraits of a Camargo, a Guimard or a Taglioni are of such interest at the present day that I will develop this with an eye to the future and risk stepping beyond the bounds of strict criticism.

3.—BACKGROUND TO THE NEW BALLET

It is important in any study of the immediate pre-War ballet period to note the extraordinary conditions under which these nomad dancers had to live, most especially before taking an individual case in some detail. They were refugees, gathered together in Paris after adventurous journeys from Russia via the ends of the earth. They had no background of comfort upon which to rely, and no sense of security. In most cases they were the breadwinners for the whole family, whose anxieties had been theirs since nursery days, and the term is wrong for they had known a studio but never a nursery.

They had done their elementary studies in French schools, though they spoke Russian at home, but neither language did they know from the point of view of literature, thought or even orthography. They lived in their trunks, the longest stay in any city being three months. They rose early for rehearsal, went to bed late. They thrived in an atmosphere of excitement, of making new friends and of saying goodbye, of success and failure, of adulation and criticism, of rivalry, misunderstanding and always of gruelling physical work. Their parents had no previous connection with the stage, and consequently were as stage struck as their own children and a good deal more bewildered. After a life spent in ordinary middle class activities followed by a spell of adventure and hardship, they seemed to be living in a dream. If these children were to know any repose, it could only be in themselves. As can be imagined, only the exceptional child reached the stage at all, many left the studios through lack of strength or will power, or more happily for marriage.

31

All this is true, but these child dancers were not unhappy nor unhealthy, and not altogether as ignorant as they might have been, for with the travel and contacts made they picked up a mass of miscellaneous and unrelated information that was gradually assimilated into their work. Life was speeded up, success came in the early teens, seasonal variation was violent. Economic conditions were largely to blame for this state of things, but a more far sighted management could have modified the worst abuses by the careful nursing of its young dancers. Never has any generation seen more brilliant material and never has material been so wasted by conditions that should never have existed. Had Monte Carlo been retained as the home of Russian emigré ballet instead of the feverish atmosphere of American tours the whole history of ballet might have taken a fresh turn.

4.—RIABOUCHINSKA *EN PANTOUFLES*

Riabouchinska is a second generation dancer and the sister of a dancer, the charming Komorova of the Diaghileff Ballet. Her father was a Moscow merchant of wealth, and like so many Moscow millionaires an enlightened patron of the arts and a man of considerable artistic culture. Her home even in the emigration never knew the want and privation suffered by her colleagues. She was a pupil first of Volinine and then of Kchessinska, to whom she owes among other things the inimitable movement of her arms. Kchessinska was also the one teacher psychologically able to instil a sense of confidence and a knowledge of stage-craft in a timid and essentially retiring nature.

It is to her mother in those formative years that Tatiana owes the most. Madame Riabouchinska was a woman of remarkable and subtle intelligence. This was her third experience of ballet, so that the great difference between Madame Riabouchinska and other stage mothers was the important fact that she knew the stage inside out and that all her stage politics were conducted according to a strict principle, the principle of try it on by all means as long as it does not interfere with the performance. I have heard her solemnly declare that Tania would positively not dance until such and such a grievance had been attended to, and then half an hour before curtain rise hustle her daughter into costume and make-up, telling her that under no circumstances does a good artist keep her public waiting. She did not, however, trouble Tania overmuch with such matters; she handled them herself and the management listened to her with considerable respect, a sort of antagonistic affection and no little awe. Mistakes she may have made, but according to her lights she played fair. She was a very gallant woman with whom it was a real pleasure to talk. Her death left a terrible void in the Company; she alone belonged to the old school. One could argue with her, disagree with her and respect her; one could be positive that her every move was to advance her daughter's career, but that in so doing she would never let the performance down. Argue heatedly until the fiddles began tuning, then action.

With her mother's death Tatiana's personality began to develop rapidly. She learned to speak up for herself and the change was immediately noticeable in her work. Even in dying when she did, Madame Riabouchinska had served her daughter's career. What Tatiana now needed was artistic not tactical guidance, and this she received from her husband, David Lichine, a magnificent critic and the biggest influence in her artistic career. He would criticise her with a frankness that I have rarely heard in the theatre, and with such guidance it was impossible for her ever to settle down into a state of complacency; the keenness of the competition was such that the slightest sign of weakening could ruin a career. Tatiana both gained and lost through having her own set rôles. Baronova and Toumanova doubled nearly every part and their rivalry not only gave them an incentive but centred most of the publicity on them. When Riabouchinska went down with scarlet fever in New York it was proved conclusively that no one else could replace her and that in her case alone the repertoire needed altering. Her gain was a certain security that gave her the freedom to concentrate on artistic improvement alone without the need of a feverish haste and strain. Physically also she was stronger by far than the majority of her colleagues.

Riabouchinska has none of the fierce ambition of her contemporaries. She is interested in the dance as a whole and in her husband's choreographic development. She is eager to foster and develop new talent and she is almost too good and sincere a colleague for the furtherance of her own career. Since the War she has been in America, but has only danced in ballet on comparatively rare occasions. Such an artist needs the stable atmosphere of an Opera House in which to shine her brightest.

(We have seen Riabouchinska once again at Covent Garden in 1947. She remains the same sensitive artist as before.)

CHAPTER VII. — BARONOVA AND TOUMANOVA

THE RIVALS

Voltaire, *balletomane,* immortalised the first great ballet rivalry in verse:

" Ah Camargo, que vous étes, brillante,
  Mais que Sallé grands dieux est ravissante,
  Que vos pas sant légers, et que les siens sout doux.
  Elle est inimitable, et vous toujours nouvelle.
  Les nymphes sautent comme vous
  Et les graces dansent comme elle."

Succeeding generations of *balletomanes* have not always shown themselves so wise, and have adopted purely partisan attitudes in which they could see but little to praise in their idol's rival. On at least one occasion in Russia the result has been a duel. Yet such rivalry has been of benefit both to ballet and the dancers themselves.

The next great rivalry was in the romantic period, that between Taglioni and Elssler, each of whom represented a different aspect of romanticism. In summing up their qualities, Gautier wrote: " Fanny Elssler's dancing . . . has a particular character which sets her apart from all other dancers; it is not the aerial and virginal grace of Taglioni, it is something more human, more appealing to the senses. Mlle. Taglioni is a Christian dancer . . . She resembles a happy angel who scarcely bends the petals of celestial flowers with the tips of her pink toes. Fanny is quite a pagan dancer . . ." *

I have already dealt at some length with the artistic personalities of Pavlova and Karsavina, as closely linked together as Camargo and Sallé, Taglioni and Elssler.

De Basil's great Russian ballet revival of 1932 (London, July 4, 1933) has added yet another pair of names to the immortals, whose rivalry may be said to have focussed the attention on ballet and marked a short but brilliant epoch.

Both girls, daughters of Russian émigrés, were trained in the Paris studio of Olga Preobrajenska, who transmitted to them the great Maryinsky tradition and a new and powerful technique that included the *pirouettes* and *fouettés* that were such a sensational feature of the pre-War ballet years. Toumanova was the first to make a name, appearing at a Pavlova gala and then at the age of eleven as a guest artist at the Paris Opéra in *L'Eventail de Jeanne.* She joined the Blum-de Basil Monte Carlo Ballet when it was formed in 1932, but left it after a season to

* Cyril Beaumont's translation.

join Edward James' *Ballets 1933*. Her departure gave Irina Baronova an opportunity to shine, and in 1933 it was Baronova who made a sensation at the Alhambra in *Les Sylphides, Les Présages, Jeux d'Enfants*, and as the midinette in *Le Beau Danube*. Toumanova rejoined de Basil later in 1933, and from then on their careers ran parallel. They shared practically every rôle for the next five years.

The conditions that existed made it impossible for any subtle criticism of their individual styles. Both dancers were overworked, under-rehearsed, and not fully mature, so that their personalities never had time to develop to the full as they would have done under more ideal conditions. It was a continual struggle not only against one another, but against a common enemy, fatigue. They varied almost from performance to performance. It might seem obvious to say that Toumanova, " the black pearl," was the more naturally dramatic, until one remembered the remarkably dramatic passion of Baronova in *Les Présages*. Baronova's range on the whole was a wider one, that included the gay and the frivolous. In pure classicism, as represented by *Aurora's Wedding*, there was very little to choose between them. At the very top of her form, Toumanova had a greater intensity of attack, while Baronova showed greater ease and fluidity. Of the two, Baronova was the more conscious artist, Toumonova the more instinctive. Between them they completely dominated a period that led to the world revival of an art that seemed to have died with Diaghileff.

The War years took them to America and to the rewards of Hollywood and Broadway, with intervals off for guest appearances in ballet. It would be interesting to have the opportunity of judging them under ideal conditions and to see how they have developed, but it is unlikely that such an opportunity will occur. Neither dancer has had the good fortune to live under conditions really worthy of their exceptional gifts.

CHAPTER VIII. — ALEXANDRA DANILOVA
AN EXAMPLE

I have dealt with the de Basil " babies " first for a definite reason. During the 1933 renaissance they largely monopolised public attention by the extraordinary scope of the new technique, as well as by their rivalry. To the connoisseur, how-ever, Alexandra Danilova occupied a unique position. She set a standard from which she never departed, she was the last ballerina who possessed the grand man-ner, whose very walk onto the stage proclaimed her position.

Danilova began her training in Imperial Russia, continued it in the arduous days of the Revolution, and came to Western Europe in the small group that followed Balanchine, or Balanchavadze, as he then was. She joined Diaghileff with him and disputed with the brilliant and erratic Nikitina the successorship to Vera Nemchinova, a ballerina whom Diaghileff failed to appreciate at her full value. When Nemchinova left, and Nikitina, in many ways too gifted, dropped out, Danilova became Diaghileff's last ballerina. She filled not only the few classical rôles of the repertoire but fitted into the new repertoire with rare dis-tinction, leaving memories of *The Triumph of Neptune, The Gods Go A'begging, Le Pas d'Acier* and *Les Matelots* that will colour the whole last period of the Rus-sian giant. Danilova's technique was never outstanding, but she had the true ballerina's breeding and an approach to the art that was fast dying out.

Few dancers have had so great an influence on the ballet of their period. When Danilova joined de Basil to start her second great career—her third is in full swing —she assumed difficulties that would have submerged the majority. She entered into direct competition with the brilliant dancers of the new generation. She not only held her own but by her example and counsel enhanced their performances. She has been the link between the new " democratic dancer " and the ballerinas of Imperial Russia.

In America, where she has been dancing since 1939, she taught the great public the meaning of style as against technique, and her example has inspired a whole generation of American dancers as it inspired the young Russians. Danilova en-joys a unique reputation at the present day, a reputation that does not fluctuate and that has not been built up by the press agent and the photographers. If other dancers are more discussed by a docile public, Danilova is always the dan-cer's dancer. It is her work that is studied and analysed not only by the aspirant but by those who have reached fame. Danilova was beginning her great career when Markova joined Diaghileff as an infant prodigy, she was at the top of her form with the emergence of Toumanova and Baronova and their generation, and she has been an example to all these dancers. She has been blessed with a sense of values that has made her one of the sole survivors of Russian ballet in America.

CHAPTER IX. — MARGOT FONTEYN

Margot Fonteyn is Britain's only prima ballerina in the correct sense of that much abused term. I believe her to be without an equal in musical and dramatic range anywhere at the present time.

Ballerinas have to be born and then they have to be made. An inch too much in height, legs that are not perfectly shaped, a large head, and the goal is unattinable whatever talent may be present. There is a ballerina type, fairly constant and easily recognisable whatever the nationality of the dancer. Given that type the intending dancer requires exceptional strength, toes that are well formed to supply a bridge that will carry the weight of the body, and a meticulous schooling that is long and scientific. Before she can dance at all she must be properly " placed " and it is there that so many born dancers are unmade. A carpenter or any true craftsman will understand that matter of " placing "; the table legs must support the weight evenly, the wood must be properly conditioned. Now come the mental and emotional gifts; a knowledge and feeling for music, resulting in a dramatic sense, poise, self confidence, quick reflexes, intelligence and a sound educational background.

Is it to be wondered at that the ballerina is a rarity, that Imperial Russia with all its resources could only produce a half dozen in a generation?

On April 24, 1946, Frederick Ashton produced at Covent Garden his ballet to César Frank's symphonic variations. It was a masterpiece of pure dancing, the prototype of which is *Les Sylphides*. It was musically subtle, rich in inventive pattern and of very great complexity for the performers, six in number, using the vast stage of the Royal Opera House. The three women were Margot Fonteyn, Pamela May and Moira Shearer. All three have appeared as Aurora in *The Sleeping Beauty,* all three are widely different in personality and physique; a brunette, a blond and a redhead. Margot Fonteyn, centrepiece of Ashton's pattern, is the most experienced, the prima ballerina upon whom the limelight has been shining for the past few years, a technician used to the diamond brilliance of the great classical variations, a personality whose habit and duty it is to attack in the grand manner and to dominate the stage. Yet Margot Fonteyn became a part of the whole, a theme in Ashton's intricate choreographic orchestration, never for a moment suggesting that this was *her* evening. To the connoisseur it was as revealing as her brio in *The Sleeping Beauty,* and even more impressive. It showed her range, her extraordinary musicianship and a sense of proportion rare on the stage. It called to mind only one other dancer of our time, Tamara Karsavina, who was always able to make herself part of a poet's conception.

The classical ballet in which the ballerina is trained sees ballet in terms of one dancer, supporting dancers and a background, while contemporary ballet calls for

37

a group of dancers supporting an idea. The dancer who is only a classical baller-ina is something of an anachronism at the present time. It is not only in the César Frank variations that Fonteyn has become a part of the pattern. As a Child of Light in the Liszt-Ashton *Dante Sonata* she does the same thing, dancing bare-footed is an entirely different idiom, showing that to the highly trained, musical and intelligent dancer Duncanism is as much within her reach as ballet. This is important since it stifles once and for all the niggling arguments of the pseudo-Grecians with their Parthenon-posings and the " modern dancers " with their ungainly, earthbound posturings.

Margot Fonteyn is in fact the very negation of acrobatics in ballet. Fonteyn is a dancer who fulfils the old poet's dictum that the great dancer is borne aloft on the arms of the music. She reacts both consciously and emotionally. She has none of the old fashioned ballerina's arrested musical development through the long habit of listening to a simple tom-tom rhythm.

Let us take a look at some of her creations and interpretations; classical, roman-tic and pure bouffe, since up to now we have dealt with the deliberate suppression of a strong personality.

Fonteyn inherited the classics from Alicia Markova, a dazzling performer with a limited dramatic range. It was Markova who had made those revivals possible and Markova whose public flocked to Sadler's Wells; a repetition in some ways of Pavlova—and her company, or so it seemed to be. When Markova left Sadler's Wells, the management was faced with a serious problem; wise planning in the school solved that problem, as it will always do.

Margot Fonteyn first made a hit in the Lambert-Ashton *Rio Grande,* an exotic water-front ballet in which she appeared as a Creole, a rôle created by Markova. It was a singularly fortunate piece of casting as a start. Markova had never ex-celled in such rôles, which were outside her range, and Fonteyn brought some-thing new to the part, one could feel the warm sun coursing through her veins, the atmosphere that was present in Lambert's music. She built a positive char-acter. There was as yet no hint that this was a ballerina. The rôles in modern ballet conceal more than they tell about a dancer's capabilities. She is always hiding behind the mask of a character. There was no doubt about her quality, however, when she made her debût later in the year in *Swan Lake*. My first *Daily Telegraph* notice bore the heading, " Newcomer in Wells Ballet—a real dis-covery," but this time I had no doubts. It was " A Rare English Ballerina — Great Performance in *Swan Lake*." Where Markova had been hard and brittle, Fonteyn stressed the romantic side. Her gesture of protecting her fellow swans from the archer, a point that always repays examination, had the true dramatic quality of fairy tale. It was no mere incident in a dancer's ballet. Her fault was a certain lack of brio in the wicked aspect of that schizzophrenic rôle and a tend-ency to the softer arms of *Les Sylphides*. This was fully conquered some years later, especially after the unromantic fireworks that are so indispensible in *Casse*

MARGOT FONTEYN

ALEXANDRA DANILOVA

YVETTE CHAUVIRE

PAULINE CLAYDEN

ANN HEATON

PEARL ARGYLE

ANNA PAVLOVA

Noisette. Her biggest test came in *Giselle* where Markova had given a brilliant second act that set a dancing standard for her contemporaries. Fonteyn's triumph was in the first act; her innocence, betrayal, insanity and suicide made the drama live as Pavlova and Spessiva had done. It was a *tour de force* where the dated music could give but little help. The famous insanity scene was built up quietly out of all that had gone before and not produced suddenly as a dazzling piece of stage hysteria. It was romantic in conception and never realistic. She did not try to make one's flesh creep but to inspire sympathy in the character. Her first act still remains her best, but the second act is now firm and the dead Giselle retains our sympathy instead of becoming just the ballerina.

The detail in her work never ceases to astonish me. In *The Sleeping Beauty,* for instance, the moment when she pricks her finger, instead of remaining an unimportant mimed incident, becomes a little drama as the spoilt child is first pained and then astonished that anything could happen to her. Each one of her classical rôles has a warm humanity added to the pure dancing and vigorous attack that make of her a ballerina. Among her most delightful portraits is that of Swanhilda in *Coppelia,* always a highly intricate rôle, demanding as fine a sense of comedy allied with brio as *Giselle* demands tragedy. So many dancers have made a success by being doll-like and pretty. With Margot Fonteyn there is no superficial interpretation. She is always the madcap Swanhilda aping the doll Coppelia, but her portrait never breaks through the rigid frame of its period, and in the last act where the demi-caractère dancer has to give place to the ballerina we see a complete change of personality. With Fonteyn we are not always conscious that we are watching Fonteyn, the ballerina. She is able to identify herself completely with each rôle. The conscious creation that goes to the building of each rôle is evident to anyone who watches her from rehearsal time, when he will see a spirited sketch, to the end of the season, when the work will have received touch after touch in order to bring it to perfection.

All this means that Fonteyn has not a touch of mannerism. To an average audience mannerism is the keynote to personality. It is certainly one of the ways in which personality is manifested, the most obvious. At times it is a highly conscious process, as when that master-showman Dolin takes the audience into his confidence, telling them exactly what he intends doing, at times it is subconscious. The uncertain dancer often gathers strength through some trick with a finger, a thrust of the jaw or even the parting of the lips into a seeming grin. On the whole, audiences fed on the crudities of the films like these things. They feel that they can always identify their favourite even when she wears a wig. Fonteyn has a vast and admiring public in spite of the fact that there is not a trace of the obvious about her. I wonder whether they always understand the full depth of her artistery? She has been dancing continuously in this country throughout the war when we have had no opportunity of seeing visiting ballerinas. This has been greatly to her disadvantage. I remember shortly before the war seeing the greatly heralded Soviet ballerina Semenova perform *Giselle* in Paris in the same week as I saw Fonteyn, not then at the full height of her powers. Semenova danced superbly, but her performance was crude beside Fonteyn's. It is only through the opportunity of making such comparisons that one can truly under- stand an artist's worth.

So far I have only discussed Fonteyn as a classicist. Her creations are rich and varied and her partnership with Frederick Ashton especially has been a fruitful one. There is the pathetic flowergirl of *Nocturne*, a great ballet with a story told in pure dancing and never for a moment obscure. There is the odd clinging female, a study in the fey, from *Wedding Bouquet*, daughter of the light in *Dante Sonata*, plastic in a manner that Wigman and her kind have never understood, and the purely burlesque dancer in *Faccade* to show an entirely new side to her character. When she took over from a succession of dancers the rôle of the sweetheart in *The Rake's Progress*, we saw it in perspective for the first time. Fonteyn brought it into alignment with the rest of the characters in Hogarth's morality. It was a period piece and she treated it as such instead of making it a charming demi-caractère interlude *sur les points*.

CHAPTER X. — MASSINE AND HELPMANN

1.—DEVELOPMENT OF THE MALE DANCER

The opposite number of the *prima ballerina,* appropriately described as the *danseur noble,* is now a thing of the past. The only dancer of that type we have seen in London was Pierre Vladimirov in Diaghileff's *Sleeping Princess* of 1921. It was Diaghileff himself with Fokine who dealt the death blow to the *danseur noble* by greatly extending the scope of male dancing. Where previously it had tended to be positively classical or positively character, Fokine filled in a hundred small shades, from the romantic, solitary man in *Les Sylphides* to the Golden Slave of *Schéhérazade* from the Spirit of the Rose to Harlequin. In truth, the rôle of the *danseur noble* was a dull one. He had to be so perfectly negative in character. The romantic ballet had almost swept him off the stage and his survival, even in Russia, was a grudging one. The ballets of Petipa contain many male variations, but we have the feeling that they exist to give the ballerina breathing space, and once she is on the stage the man drops into the background. He lifts her, he indicates to the audience his rapture at her grace and beauty, and that is all. Dramatically his rôle is strictly negative. True he may be a heroic prince, but that aspect is never developed. In *The Sleeping Beauty,* for instance, he is entirely a lay figure. We are introduced to him out hunting; then the Lilac Fairy comes to show him a vision of the enchanted Aurora. Under the tutelage of good governess Lilac Fairy he dances with this vision and is then led through the wood and into the castle where he kisses the Princess. That is the end of his dramatic rôle. For the rest of the ballet he becomes the partner of a pas de deux in a divertissement. Could any man be more hen-pecked? First by his good fairy-in-law and then by his wife. In *Swan Lake* also, while the man's rôle is slightly more prominent, he and his friends are singularly passive at the great moment of the Adagio. Yet, while these male rôles of classical ballet are singularly passive, they call for rare qualities in physique and training. If the *danseur noble* has little opportunity of shining on his own account, the ballerina's great triumph is certainly largely due to his handling of her and, if he is less than adequate, he can entirely ruin her effect. His work, therefore, is noted and appraised by the expert rather than by the general public. In *Giselle,* not strictly speaking a classical ballet at all, his part is far more conspicuous and he requires to be a good romantic actor in order to carry any conviction. But even here it is an absurdity to call this the Hamlet of male rôles, as has so often been done. The dramatic emphasis is entirely on the ballerina. An adequate male will not ruin *Giselle,* but the ballerina must be very much more than adequate to make this old-fashioned work live and have a meaning at the present day.

45

How admirably Fokine understood the true rôle of the male dancer. *Les Syl-phides* is an example of that. The man there is not merely the conventional part-ner of classical ballet. He has a positive contribution to make and the pas de deux is truly a pas de deux, completely removed, both in feeling and technique, from the *Swan Lake* Adagio. This male rôle in *Les Sylphides* has all too rarely been danced well, so that it tends to be misunderstood. There is always a con-fusion between the romantic male and the effeminate male. The solitary man in *Les Sylphides* is essentially romantic and also essentially virile; although there is no story, he is as much the lover as the Prince in any of the enchanted glades of classical ballet. Also his male technique is an essential part of the orchestration. Imagine *Les Sylphides* without the male rôle, and the result would be merely a very pretty series of dances from a pantomime. The same is the case with *Le Spectre de la Rose*. What a bold imagination to make this spirit of a flower into a man, and how complex the resulting rôle that calls for tenderness and athletic-ism.

This extension of the male rôle in ballet does not mean that the need for the *danseur noble* has vanished. For a long time Diaghileff dispensed with the classics, so that he was largely forgotten, but now when the classics form a large part of every programme it has become almost impossible to replace him, since once a man has been trained in the very positive rôles of the modern repertoire he can no longer sink into something so purely passive.

Nijinsky represented the new male dancer, with a range that had hitherto been unknown, and it is for that reason, as well as for his genius as a dancer, that his name belongs to history. We have to go back to the days of Vestris before an-other man joins the glorious roll of balletic fame. After Nijinsky there is no longer anything strange in a man occupying his fair share of the limelight.

By far the most interesting contemporary male dancers are Leonide Massine and our own Robert Helpmann. Neither of them can be definitely classified since their range is so extensive. Both are highly creative; both excel in depicting character.

2.—LEONIDE MASSINE—THE LAST OF THE GIANTS

Leonide Massine's vast range includes everything but the purely classical from which his physique and temperament exclude him. His romantic interpretations include the poet Eusebius in *Carnaval* and the Prince in the *Firebird*. The first rôle is largely misunderstood at the present day and we realise what a lot it con-tains when we compare Massine's performance to that of his successors. His Eusebius was a true poet of that period. By far his finest romantic rôle is that of the Hussar in his own *Beau Danube*. This ballet might so easily have been the conventional synthetic Viennese product. The elegance that it calls for is

46

obvious but Massine made it into a true character. I know of few moments more thrilling than when he walks on to the stage and throws his shako into the wings. This has true gaiety with none of the forced " Let's be Viennese at all costs " atmosphere, so very familiar to frequenters of the films or operettes. Another truly memorable moment is when Massine stands in the centre of the stage while the characters pass him by in scorn. Usually there is no more helpless creature than the dancer when he stands motionless. Massine made that lack of motion into something positive and eloquent. In his masterpiece, *The Three Cornered Hat,* there is that same gaiety and a complete identification of himself with the character that he impersonates. The actual Farucca may have been better danced by Leon Woizikovsky, an outstanding character dancer, but it largely remained a brilliant dance, while Massine showed the breeding of the Spanish peasant and the feeling of mischief for which the plot called. His Petrouchka was on the whole less successful since one was always a little too aware of his human intelligence and could not altogether believe that he would find himself in such a situation. In his long series of grotesques there are many variations, from the *rasta* Parisian Can-Can dancer, who has almost walked out of a canvas by Lautrec, to the Chaplin-esque Barman in *Union Pacific,* a weak ballet that only gains humanity when he is on the stage. In *Gaiet Parisienne* his Peruvian visitor to Paris has all the period gusto of Offenbach's music. What a sharp contrast between the Can-Can Dancer and the Peruvian! Massine's powerful personality does not intrude in such a way that every rôle is assimilated into it. He is an admirable servant of Massine the choreographer. His keen intelligence seems to electrify the stage and always there is the feeling that he has still more in reserve, the test of all great artists.

Since his rise to fame immediately after the 1914-18 War, Massine has been the dominating figure not only as dancer but as choreographer, and though he is no longer young his particular gifts should shine in ballet for a very long time to come; the purely athletic side of his dancing matters far less than with the average male. He can be measured by no ordinary standards. It is indeed fortunate that our young dancers have had an opportunity of working with the last of the giants.

3.—ROBERT HELPMANN

Robert Helpmann occupies very much the same rôle in our British Ballet as does Massine with the Russian, though his range includes the classical. I have never been able to answer the obvious question: Is Helpmann a good classical dancer? I rather suspect that he is not, judged by the standard of the past. His rôle as a classical dancer may well depend on his abilities as an actor. He is certainly convincing and inspires immediate confidence as he steps on to the stage,

47

Ninette de Valois in a masterly summary writes: " to me he represents a perfect example of a dancer in which facility and talent meet on equal terms, and at a very high rate of exchange. His technical acquisition does not follow the virtuosity lines of spectacular execution, but favours that form representing perfection of detail in both simple and complex movements." It would be difficult to improve on that. He has the same authority and positive quality as Massine when he is not in motion. Also his handling of the difficult and easily dated mime is magnificent. We do not feel that these gestures have all been learned by rote, but that they are a part of the dance instead of a rather trying interruption in which the story must be hastily told. He is genuinely moved by the beauty and the plight of his Princess. If he is not the complete danseur noble, and physically he falls short of the rôle, he is an admirable substitute, who thinks and feels in terms of the period. This is as much a dramatic feat as the more obvious character parts such as the Rake or Mr O'Reilly.

From the Prince to Doctor Coppelius is a very long journey. Helpmann's Coppelius may not please those who insist on a rigid adherence to tradition in which every gesture is laid down and performed in the same way by every interpreter of the rôle. Helpmann has humanised the figure and in that respect has taken it out of its classical framework. He has not, however, except on the rare occasions when an exuberant audience inspires him to gag and over-act, destroyed the fabric of the work. While tradition in ballet is all important, I have little sympathy with those who expect the gestures and expressions of sixty years ago to remain unvaried. If a ballet has any right to survive, then its rôles must be continually re-discovered as are the great rôles of the dramatic stage. To deny that would be to reduce the dancer to the rôle of a marionette. The only question is one of degree and on that opinion must differ.

Helpmann is essentially a man of the theatre who revels in trapdoors, wigs and character make-ups, and he looks at his dancing rôles primarily from that point of view. It is not only a different conception from that of the average dancer but also from that of a Massine himself.

CHAPTER XI. — SOME BRITISH DANCERS

THE BACKGROUND

I have traced the background of British Ballet in previous volumes.* Since these were written the pattern has become more definite, the National Ballet truly exists. Sadler's Wells is distinguished from any other non-state company by reason of its school, its second company allowing room for experiment and the stability of its constitution. Those factors are vital at the present day. Diaghileff's great strength, apart from his personality, lay in the fact that his ballet had a home, Monte Carlo, that he could draw on the finest Russian schools, and that being alone in the field he had stability. These facts should always be borne in mind. Diaghileff was remarkable in so many directions that it is impossible to attempt to imitate him or to name a successor, but it is not only possible but necessary to study the conditions under which he worked and to realise the different economic conditions that prevailed. The Diaghileff Ballet was never a business, it was never intended to pay and it never could have paid. Diaghileff as a consequence was entirely free to select his programmes and his cast and to launch those dancers in whom he believed without paying the slightest attention to any impresario or his press agent. That to-day is the position of our own ballet, though it must pay its way since Maecenas has been dead these many years. It must pay its way, but for all that it is in no sense a commercial organisation, enriching certain individuals. It is the typical British compromise between Diaghileff's freedom and a national institution. As such it forms the perfect background for the development of the young dancer.

1.—PAMELA MAY AND JUNE BRAE

When in 1935 Sadler's Wells began to show its true individuality, two dancers in particular attracted special attention; June Brae and Pamela May. They have had curiously parallel careers, sharing rôles, retiring from the stage for a period and now making a very welcome return.

In many respects Pamela May has been the most classical dancer in pure line that the company has produced. An early Blue Bird of hers has yet to be equalled, and it is in such rôles that she excels rather than in the sustaining and development of a ballerina part. That is not to say that she lacks the necessary equipment but that she sometimes fails in intensity of attack or in concentration so that she cannot always bring the rôle to a satisfactory dramatic climax. Where

* The National Ballet (A. & C. Black).

49

Pamela May excels is in the gay and lighthearted, whether it be in a creation such as the Dancer in *The Prospect Before Us* or the soubrette of Swanhilda in *Coppelia,* where her performance is a joy. Pamela May is essentially a soubrette. But she is not confined within such narrow limits. Outstanding was her Red Queen in *Checkmate* and her Moon in *Horoscope.*

June Brae has never possessed a very strong technical equipment from a purely classical point of view. Her gifts have been lyrical and dramatic and she has shown them to perfection in two contrasting rôles, her creation of the Black Queen in *Checkmate* and as the Lilac Fairy in *The Sleeping Beauty* (first Wells production). Her intoxicated Josephine in *Wedding Bouquet* also remains a delightful memory. Since her return June Brae may have lost in technique but she has gained in maturity. Her numerous rôles in *Adam Zero,* particularly her dance as Death, call for the same intensity as in *Checkmate.* She succeeds in them all, save when as the dancer she has to perform some rather conventional ballet. In *Assembly Ball* her style and personality triumph over weak dancing and she is able to dominate the scene and bring some climax to a ballet that seems over long without her. Where June Brae excels is in her musicality. Her *prélude* in *Les Sylphides* is outstanding for that reason.

May and Brae, once so closely linked together, have now taken entirely new directions. They represent a very important and critical phase in the development of our ballet, the emergence of individuals from a *corps de ballet,* the beginnings of artistry. Their experience and the gifts they have developed are valuable at the present time.

2.—BERYL GREY

Beryl Grey has an ease and fluency that are altogether exceptional. She inspires immediate confidence in the most difficult technical rôles. Her line is superb. Her height alone gives cause for anxiety. Height is the great enemy of the intending bellerina, but at the same time the whole question has become greatly exaggerated. There is nothing displeasing about a tall dancer, if she is a fine dancer. On the contrary her line will be accentuated, and for that reason both her faults and her virtues will be more evident. The difficulties involved are practical rather than aesthetic, how to find a partner of the right height and strength. The tall dancer must be of exceptional quality to reach the front rank. Beryl Grey undoubtedly has such quality. Her dancing is not merely naturally graceful, but shows considerable thought in its presentation. Few dancers correct faults with such speed, improving from performance to performance. Beryl Grey is very naturally, at the moment, more developed as a dancer than as an artist, but in her many interpretations there is nothing to eliminate.

They only require the detailed additions that experience can bring. Her range —considerations of height apart—brings the promise of being an extended one, judging by her very striking Duessa in the *Quest, Dante Sonata* and, to me, her altogether outstanding *Les Sylphides*. As Aurora in *The Sleeping Beauty,* her ease was amazing, especially in the *Rose Adagio,* that the word *attack* seems out of place, but it was a performance that carried right up to the back of the balcony.

Beryl Grey is one of the few among our dancers to start as a prodigy. At the age of fifteen she was dancing ballerina rôles, replacing at very short notice an injured Margot Fonteyn. Sadlers Wells does not as a rule encourage the infant phenomenon, but in this case the need was absolute. It reflects enormous credit both on the dancer and the system that she has not developed the slightest trace of mannerism.

I sometimes wonder where those rabid ballet lovers of pre-war years who fêted and applauded the amazing young Russians have gone. They have missed an episode that they would have found greatly to their liking in the emergence and development of Beryl Grey.

3.—MOIRA SHEARER

Ballet lovers are anything if not wildly enthusiastic. They may know that the true ballerina appears but once within a decade, but yet they are full of hope every time the curtain rises. Every goose is a swan until she has proved the contrary beyond the shadow of a doubt. This atmosphere of wishful thinking makes the older critic—who has been a wishful thinker in his day—doubly wary. He knows that no dancer leaps to fame in a single performance or for that matter in a single season. She creeps to fame laboriously after a year or two of ups and downs. She must prove herself in a number of rôles, not modern creations but those test pieces in which she must measure herself against memories of the great.

During the first record-breaking Sadler's Wells season at Covent Garden, a young Titian-haired dancer, Moira Shearer, caused a balletic sensation by her dancing of the ballerina rôle in *The Sleeping Beauty*. She made her debut, as is usual in such cases, at a matinée and then danced it at evening performances, fourteen times in all; sure sign of a very great success. Her outstanding beauty may have been an advantage in focussing the public attention. It could also have been a handicap had she lacked the ability to exploit it properly. Exactly how well—glamour apart—did Shearer dance the rôle of Aurora? Is her future as dazzling as some enthusiasts believe?

But first let us take a closer look at Moira Shearer, tracing some of the steps before she found herself the centre of the stage at Covent Garden.

Moira Shearer was born in 1926 in Carnegie's town of Dunfermline. At the age of six she left with her parents for Rhodesia, and there at Ndola, near the Belgian

Congo of all places, she met a dancer who had been in the Diaghileff Company and who gave her her first lessons. The little girl was promising—all little girls are—and she was enthusiastic. She returned to Scotland for three years during which she continued her general education with a Scottish thoroughness and then came to London. She had been sent to Legat by her first Russian teacher, and after a few months with Flora Fairbairn he took her on. After the master's death she studied for four years with Madame Legat. She then joined the Sadler's Wells school, but the War had started, and, after six weeks, to her great disgust, she was evacuated to Scotland, thoroughly miserable at leaving the dance. Her stage debût was with the International Ballet, and the engagement lasted for a year. In 1942 she joined Sadler's Wells where she has been ever since.

So far a perfectly ordinary career except that it was one devoid of the customary academic distinctions for which the young dancer had not the slightest ambition. She attracted immediate attention on account of her looks and found the many references to " the lovely redhead " intensely annoying. She was and is ambitious, but ambitious for success through her dancing and interpretation. Her background was a musical one, and it was natural for her to see dancing not merely in terms of steps, the sole goal of so many youngsters. Lack of time made her give up the piano, but she was well grounded and able to see the connection between the two arts. At Sadlers Wells the musical aspect of ballet is greatly stressed. Her first creations were in *The Quest,* the *pas de trois* in *Promenade,* and one of the lovers in *Miracle in the Gorbals.* In this last she was brilliantly cast, and the lyrical element in her work stood out of the drab and vicious slum background. It was in the prélude of *Les Sylphides,* acid test of artistry, that she first attracted my attention. It was a beautifully sensitive performance, romantic and without a trace of false sentiment. It did not occur to me that she could possibly possess the technique, authority or attack to make anything of a showing in a great classical rôle.

At Covent Garden Moira Shearer showed an altogether unsuspected self-confidence. She stepped out onto the stage like a conqueror with none of the apologetics of the beginner. If she made a mistake—and of course there were several—she summoned up an astonishing degree of stage-craft to mask it. Only the expert could notice a slight strain of the mouth that revealed nervous anxiety. " I was petrified, shaking like a jelly," she said. " I had no idea that I was giving an impression of self-confidence." With repeated performances Shearer improved the detail of the work. If it remained technically imperfect, the manner of its presentation and its musicality were truly impressive.

For Moira Shearer's sake let us not be guilty of any exaggeration. It is impossible for at least another year to say whether she will reach the top and gain like Fonteyn before her, not merely technical precision but true mastery of artistic detail. The " ifs " are so many, but much depends on her own reaction to this altogether unusual success.

In character, Moira Shearer is given to extremes of optimism or pessimism. She is temperamental in the manner of the young Russian dancers of whom she reminds me in so many ways. She will not, I believe, succumb to flattery, and she has some hard things to say of the fans and followers who see in every temporary success a permanent triumph. Also, *Red Shoes* apart, she has resisted many tempting offers from films and commercial theatres, realising that at this stage they would be fatal. Yet she has ambitions as an actress, " if and when I reach the top of the tree as a dancer. I do not draw such a sharp distinction between these two branches of the theatre, to do so would be to make dancing seem too mechanical. It is my ambition one day to act in Shaw. I fully realise that the offers I am receiving just now have nothing to do with my capabilities. Before I took up acting I would need a very thorough training. There is plenty of time, but meanwhile all my thoughts lie in perfecting myself as a dancer."

Her interests apart from dancing lie in languages, for which she has a marked aptitude, and in reading. She has a taste for history and historical novels, as befits a romantic from the land of Walter Scott. Her intelligence and integrity, her ambition which is regulated by a cold and dogged judgment, all give one reason to hope—and this reserve is the result of a very long experience—that, the film industry permitting, in Moira Shearer our National Ballet has found yet another dancer of International status.

3.—JULIA FARRON

Julia Farron is one of the most interesting and intelligent *demi-caractère* and character dancers in ballet to-day, the type of artist that Diaghileff would have admired.

She started her ballet career full of academic honours and was being groomed as a ballerina. Those early classical performances had great promise, but they revealed marked mannerisms where the story itself called for the acting of no definite rôle. Those " startled nymph " performances were piquante, elegant and full of interest. They were never truly classical. In build, also, Farron was losing the particular ballerina type.

It is a moot point how far temperament and physique march together. I have often seen the physically unsuited dancer long for the classics, but rarely the reverse. The purely classical build usually carries with it the classical temperament. What is excessively rare, however, is for a dancer who has traced out a definite path for herself to go back and follow an entirely new line with success. Farron has accomplished this after a comparatively short period in which she seemed to lose her way and stand still.

Her first *demi-caractère* interpretation of note was as Estrella in *Carnaval*. No ballet has tended to fade more rapidly than this. *Carnaval* was never a great work. It was conceived for a special occasion, a charity ball, and designed for the ballroom. Diaghileff rescued it with little real enthusiasm at first and it came to magnificent life because of its superb casting of Karsavina and Nijinsky and their contemporaries. It is a fragile period piece in which every rôle must be danced with true understanding, an understanding that it is difficult for the contemporary dancer to possess. Since Idzikovski, the rôle of Harlequin has almost disappeared, Ursula Moreton is the last true Chiarina that I can remember. Columbine still survives in Fonteyn. Eusebius vanished with Massine's youth, Pantalon is but a ghost. Farron's Estrella brought back the original flavour of *Carnaval* and immediately revealed her quality. It was not merely danced but acted, and such acting calls for a real sense of style. Farron has a remarkable sense of style. Her Queen in *The Sleeping Beauty* may have been too young to possess sufficient authority, but it had the makings of a very fine rôle.

Farron's finest work has been in *Miracle in the Gorbals*. She stood out from the first as a woman of the streets, later to shine in the leading rôle of The Prostitute, inherited from Celia Franca. And what a brazen baggage she creates, how she flaunts herself in front of the Minister, proud of her body, eager for conquest. It is a perfect study, magnificently realistic but always within the framework of ballet. Sudden conversion is always difficult to convey in the theatre, but Farron's Magdalen is absolutely sincere and convincing, a character from a novel by Dostoievsky.

Here then are examples of Farron's work from two ends of the dramatic scale; a figure in porcelain and a piece of battered earthenware, Estrella and the Prostitute. In between, the dancer who started her career as the faithful dog in *Wedding Bouquet* has many interesting portraits. I find her white skater in Ashton's ever delightful *Les Patineurs* an especial favourite. It has a bite that the more purely classical dancers lack, it is closer to its period and to the music of Meyerbeer that sets these skaters in motion.

A dancer such as Farron can rest assured of a long and important career in ballet.

4.—PAULINE CLAYDEN

There are certain artists whom it is exceedingly difficult to place, they refuse to be given one of the customary labels so convenient to the critic. Tatiana Riabouchinska, as we have seen, was an outstanding example of such a dancer. Pauline Clayden, who shares many gifts with the great Russian, is another case in point. She stresses in her work the ephemeral; Papillon in *Carnaval,* the Humming Bird in *The Sleeping Beauty,* the Suicide in *Miracle in the Gorbals,* the Nymph in the Glade in *Les Sylphides.* This impression is created partly through physique, partly through temperament, but also through a lack of technical strength. She resembles one of those truly musical singers with a voice of great purity but one that lacks the power required to sing heroic rôles or to ring the changes in coloratura fashion. I have seen the prélude in *Les Sylphides* infinitely better danced, but I have seldom seen it interpreted more movingly or with a greater feeling that here was something infinitely fragile, something that at cockscrow would vanish into the morning mist. Here, if only the necessary strength existed, is a possible second act in *Giselle,* but it is still a long journey from Fokine's romanticism to Coralli's classicism even though the emotional link be evident.

In her creation of The Suicide, Clayden is deeply moving. Certain moments are outstanding where the drowned girl feels the blood beginning to flow in her veins and turns from spiritual ecstasy to physical joy.

Rightly cast, Pauline Clayden has a quality that is rare in any dancer, a fragment of the Pavlova of *Valse Triste* and the *Californian Poppy*.

5.—MARGARET DALE

On a memorable occasion a child who might have wandered straight out of the school playground brought the curtain down on a ballet performance with the words, " But he's got nothing on." This rather shocking innovation was the climax to a shortlived work, *The King's New Clothes*. The speaker was Margaret Dale.

From the first Margaret Dale attracted attention by her strong personality and the feeling that she had an intense desire to succeed. There was in her determination at a time when her physique did not suggest success more than a hint of those qualities that had placed Preobajenska in the very front rank—wit, eagerness and an intelligence that informed all her work. As Sabrina in *Comus* she created a rôle that suited her particular style, and since then she has had a number of successes both in classical and soubrette rôles.

Margaret Dale has true intelligence and a finely developed sense of the stage. She comes out as a conqueror, attacks and keeps plenty in reserve for a brilliant climax. Her stagecraft is skilled in the extreme, and the customary British fault of a slightly apologetic air in the case of any technical mishap is quite foreign to her. If her brilliance is sometimes faked, the imitation is first class. She has true *brio* as she reveals in *Casse Noisette* or The Blue Bird. She inspires applause and by no unworthy tricks. She thoroughly deserves it. I have never yet seen her give a lackadaisical performance.

55

The male dancer is the Achilles heel of the British dancing body. It has become so much the fashion to decry our male dancers, especially since the advent of the French and Americans, that we are apt to lose all sense of proportion and the whole matter requires careful investigation. It is always dangerous in such matters to follow a fashion blindly. It was once the fashion to accuse all our dancers of a lack of temperament. The fashion died hard.

Ballet at the time of its birth and childhood was dominated by the male dancer. He gradually lost his supremacy with the emergence of the ballerina, and during the romantic period of Taglioni, Cerrito, Ellsler, Grahn and Crisi he suffered almost complete extinction. In Russia alone did he survive, partly through the connection with serfdom and partly through the possession of many vigorous forms of national dance. Serge Diaghileff, through Fokine, restored the natural balance, and the first startling success of his ballet in Western Europe was gained by the essentially male Prince Igor and by the dancer Adolf Bolm. Then the brilliance of Nijinsky brought back the vogue for the classical *danseur noble* as opposed to the character dancers.

It must not be imagined, however, that the *danseur noble* was ever anything but exceptional. If we think of the great male names of Russian ballet, they were nearly all character dancers: Mordkin, Massine, Woizikovski, Idzikovski, who was on the borderline of classicism, and the later dancers Lichine, Shabelevsky, Lazovsky. The three outstanding classical dancers were Vladimiroff, Volinine and Wilzak, all of whom were overshadowed by great ballerinas. It is therefore an error to imagine that there is such a great falling off in classical male dancers. As to the character dancers, considered apart from the mimes, the outstanding ones have been Poles or Russians, which is perfectly understandable since both nations have a strong dance tradition which does not exist in England. Our male mimes at the present day are as good as any, and with a wide range from the realism of a Beggar in *Miracle in the Gorbals* to the stylised Dr Coppelius.

Our first male classical dancer was Anton Dolin, whose career ran parallel with that of the Russian, Serge Lifar. While under the discipline and artistic guidance of Diaghileff, both men gave performances that placed them in the very front rank. Dolin in the *Blue Train* was a pioneer of the acrobatic classicism that has recently amazed and delighted us in Jerome Robbins' *Fancy Free*. His Blue Bird of 1925, especially when danced with Vera Savina, remains as the memory of a standard that has not been reached since. His partnering was, with the exception of Wilzak's, the finest I have seen. When Dolin left Diaghileff—and the same applies to Lifar—his performances varied from day to day. At times we saw the true *danseur noble* and at others a brilliant music hall performer striving for and usually gaining great applause. His position in the history of ballet has been of importance, both in this country and in the United States. Greater taste added to his fine physique, his bold attack and his undoubted intelligence might have made him a still bigger figure. Dolin ranks as an Anglo-Russian, and apart from his leadership of his own company, which was comparatively shortlived, his direct influence on our main ballet development has been small. His influence in the United States has been far more direct.

It was Harold Turner who became our first British male classical dancer and who played the biggest rôle in the development of our ballet from the classical male point of view, as a glance at the Rambert and later the Wells repertoires will clearly show. Turner possesses a fine virile technique and is at the same time a very good artist in the creation of those dramatic rôles that do not call for excessive subtlety. It must be remembered that he was chosen at a very early age to dance *Le Spectre de la Rose* with Karsavina. At about the same time as Turner another dancer, Walter Gore, revealed an entirely masculine gift of great charm and personality, and he has continued to develop though he lacks a certain intensity of attack.

At the outbreak of War, Sadlers Wells possessed such dancers as Michael Somes, Jack Hart, Richard Ellis and Alan Carter, all of whom were as yet immature but who had great promise. It was in the male ranks that our ballet suffered the greatest damage. No sooner did a boy show promise than he was whisked off to the Army and his place taken by a raw and immature youth. There was a total change in the male ranks of our ballet. Our men fought in all theatres of war. And the same thing continues at the present moment. In addition, male dancing is heavy work, and the dietary available is in every way insufficient. Much of what is styled effeminacy is in reality immaturity.

All the foregoing is not presented by way of apology but as an explanation. I do not, however, suggest that all is well with our male dancing. When there is no national dancing in a country there can be no real tradition of male dancing, and as a consequence the wrong type of boy is often attracted to ballet and thinks of it too much in terms of grace than athleticism. It takes time and the example of a number of the right type of dancers to build such a tradition. Present conditions hinder, if they do not make impossible, such an outcome, at anyrate for the next few years.

A possible solution is the teaching of boys by males from a very early age. That would effect a great change. It is a solution, but from where are these male teachers to come? It is in such practical matters that the critic so often fails.

Alexis Rassine, a South African of Russian parentage, has the perfect build for classical dancing and has in many performances shown that he can dance really well. He has only occasionally stepped definitely over the line that separates the promising dancer from the accomplished dancer. I have rarely seen anyone vary so greatly from performance to performance. Whether his failures when they take place are due to a lack of self-confidence or a lack of concentration, it is difficult to decide. His Albert in *Giselle* was a really fine performance in spite of the fact that it was undertaken at very short notice. It avoided those excesses of acting that so frequently disfigure the rôle. His young lover in *Miracle in the Gorbals* was also admirable, and his bridegroom in *The Foolish Virgins* truly belonged to its Renaissance setting. In Blue Bird his ups and down have been the greatest, yet here is a rôle that his physique demands. As a partner he tends to be uncertain and does not always inspire the confidence that is essential in double work, yet the faults do not in any case arise out of a lack of taste or a desire to steal the limelight.

David Pattenghi has filled a number of rôles of very wide dramatic range with very real distinction. I have indeed never seen him give an indifferent interpretation though his actual dancing is technically limited. In the classics he has all the allure of the *danseur noble*, and his strong build makes him a fine opposite to Beryl Grey. It is in two creations in particular that he shows his quality to the full. In *Miracle in the Gorbals* he presents the minister as a complete character in whom it is possible to divine motives, to see both a good and a bad side, while as the stage manager in *Adam Zero* one has the feeling that this man of quiet efficiency is truly controlling not only the actual performance but the destinies of the characters themselves. In all his acting, whether it be as Doctor Coppelius or as Hilarion, Patenghi shows a fine restraint and a real grasp of balletic acting whose very essence is restraint, the remaining within the framework of music and choreography, the expression of an emotion with the body rather than the face. In his classical mime as well, Patenghi is convincing. He has been a pillar of strength to the company.

It would be unfair to deal with those dancers who have recently returned from the Forces, or with the youngsters who have yet to find themselves. I cannot, knowing the full facts, take a too pessimistic view of British male dancing. It should show within the next ten years—and how short a time where ballet is concerned—a really marked improvement.

To sum up; the classical male dancer has been a rarity for many years and to-day there is not such a great falling off in his numbers. De Basil at the peak of his effort could present no opposite number to Danilova, Toumanova and Baronova; he did possess a fine number of character dancers. The character dancer is essentially the product of a country rich in folk dancing. To compensate for this we need the example of a few vigorous and mature males. Conditions make this impossible. Finally, there are insufficient male teachers in England.

If, then, knowing these facts, we take the recent production of *The Sleeping Beauty* with the great male strength required, we cannot call the standard as depressingly low as some critics would make out.

MOIRA SHEARER

TATIANA RIABOUCHINSKA

PAMELA MAY

CHAPTER XIII. — BRITISH DANCERS: THE FUTURE

When writing of the contemporary dancer there is almost the certainty that any criticism will date almost from season to season. Faults are eliminated, and it is only when the dancer becomes set that faults develop into mannerisms. The most difficult dancer of all to criticise is the adolescent who so often reveals what is a wholly deceptive appearance of conscious artistry. For that reason I have avoided as much as possible any discussion of the novice, and even when dealing with the more mature dancer I have tried to stick to general principles, avoiding the mention of technicalities that are being closely watched by those in authority.

There can be no doubt from what we have seen in the Wells second company that our young dancers are full of promise. The young dancers of the de Basil Ballet were no better equipped than Anne Heaton, Nadia Nerina, Sheila O'Reilly or Donald Britton, but just because I hope that our dancers are being more carefully handled I will refrain from a discussion of their work at the moment. Anything that I might say would be or should be speedily out of date. They have re-created and created a number of rôles in a remarkable manner. Anne Heaton in *The Gods Go A'begging, Mardi Gras, Promenade* and *Les Sylphides,* Nadia Nerina in *Mardi Gras,* and Sheila O'Reilly in *Khadra,* all show unusual gifts that wise treatment will develop and that premature exploitation could ruin within a season. They have benefited by the system, and by the tradition that has already sprung up. There now exists the machinery to make the most of their talent.

There is still, however, a dearth of good dancers in proportion to the number who learn. There can be no disguising the fact that, outside a handful of teachers, not all of whom live in London, the standard of teaching in Britain is disgracefully low. Too many talented children are wasted and their dancing teachers are quite unsuited to collaborate with their school teachers, an absolute essential.* The average teacher has no conception of ballet and only knows the mispronounced names of a few isolated steps and movements. Alongside the art of ballet there exists a great dancing industry run by women who have neither the knowledge to impart nor the example by which they can inspire. This is a very serious matter and one that cannot be remedied for some time to come. Yet the remedy does exist. Our ballet will in time produce experienced teachers from its own ranks and in its Teachers' Training Course the Royal Academy of Dancing aims at producing teachers with a definite vocation rather than thwarted dancers. Post-Diaghileff *ballet russe* relied almost exclusively on four teachers: Preobrajenska, Kchesinska, Egorova and Volinine, but they were accomplished artists of exceptional experience. We cannot rely on the possession of such teachers, but we can and must erect the necessary machinery to ensure that less talent is wasted. Sadlers Wells has proved once again that the school is the very soul of a company.

* See " The Making of a Dancer " (A. & C. Black).

1.—THE BACKGROUND

Russian (émigré) ballet, conveniently styled *ballet-russe* by Prince Lieven, set the standard of present day ballet first through Serge Diaghileff and later through Colonel de Basil. Diaghileff brought perfection of detail and drew upon the greatest artistic talent in matters of production. De Basil showed a popularisation of the Diaghileff formula and introduced a vast new public to the art. With Diaghileff the artistic ensemble was of the first importance. With de Basil the prowess and personality of the individual dancer.

The absence of *ballet-russe* from Europe during the War and the commercial conditions pertaining in America have led to its decay and to the development of various national movements arising out of it.

In Britain our movement comes direct from Diaghileff and Cecchetti via de Valois, Rambert, and, in music, Lambert. In France through Serge Lifar, the supreme influence that did much to revive a moribund art, and through Boris Kochno, a very considerable artist, and in actual dancing through the pre-Diaghileff ballerinas, Preobrajenska, Kchesinska and Egorova, and through Boris Kniaseff.

In America the Russian influence has been equally marked. Teachers have included Fokine, Bolm, Mordkin, Semenoff, Novikoff, Vladimiroff, Obouhoff, and, of a later generation, Wilzak, Schollar, Nemchinova, and especially Balanchine, brought there by the energetic and cantankerous Lincoln Kirstein to whom American ballet owes an especial debt. It is, however, not only those teachers that have had a great formative influence but also the impact of Colonel de Basil's Company on the American pubilc. When he came to the St James' Theatre in December, 1933, ballet in America seemed a lost cause. None of the teachers had done much good save to themselves in the matter of fees. They had formed no ballet and their many pupils pirouetted ad nauseam on the Roxy and other stages. That the American had an extraordinary physical and rhythmic aptitude no one who had seen Patricia Bowman or Harriet Hoctor could doubt. But that aptitude was being wasted on tricks and stunts. The artistic dance in America did not descend from the traditional ballet at all but from the many pupils of Ruth St Denis. These " modern " dancers must not be confused with the barbarities of Wigman and the central Europeans. They had and they have within their limits something interesting and original to offer to a restricted pubilc. Colonel de Basil, through the backing of his powerful impresario, S. Hurok, altered, within two seasons, the whole status of ballet. He stimulated dancers and public and almost immediately inspired others; Lincoln Kirstein with his American Ballet and later Ballet Caravan and Catherine Littlefield with her Philadelphia Ballet.

The very success of *ballet-russe* brought about its downfall. The whole strategy of the campaign was a tragic error. Publicity was centred on a few individuals at the expense of the whole. People did not go so much to see a ballet as to see Mlle. X in a ballet. The natural consequence was that Mlle. X and her companions, Mlles. Y and Z, gained a market value, and began to be quoted as stocks and shares. The annual contracts stipulated for their presence, and Broadway and Hollywood became very conscious of their existence. Life on the road with one-night-stands was hard and not very rewarding. Mlles. X, Y and Z very naturally preferred to remain in the big cities. They left the ballet to become guest artists in New York, Chicago and Los Angeles. The rest of the time the big rôles were danced by members of the company. It would be difficult to imagine a more disruptive system. The management became a slave to its artists, losing complete control of casting, programme making and even of fresh productions. Inevitably one company became two. More and more splits developed until there were three or four major companies and any amount of concert groups exploiting personalities for all they were worth. The Diaghileff principle was dead, the press agent ruled in his place. The original Russian element was by now so diluted that *ballet-russe* was dead in fact, if not yet in name.

This possibly may have been an admirable opportunity for the native American dancer and choreographer. It can be turned to artistic profit so long as the star system is totally abolished and the companies gain stability and the time and atmosphere in which to create. The one-night-stand is a barbarous institution. The public in these one-performance-cities are so little ballet-minded that everything to them must have the Russian Ballet label, must be " the biggest and the best " in true Ringling brothers fashion. The performances that they see, judging by some I witnessed before the War, are a disgrace. No city that cannot support ballet for the minimum period of a week is worth a visit. Is it to be wondered at with these conditions that dancers grow weary of ballet and sigh for a long run in a Broadway musical, an experience detrimental to their art and outlook, however good the choreography?

That then is the background against which to view the American dancer: fine teaching, magnificent physique and aptitude, no belief in a stable management, overwork that is unproductive and a lack of the feeling of tradition in the classics, which are voted boring in quantity unless danced in tabloid form by one of the much boosted stars. In addition to that the *ballet-russe* repertoire grows paler month by month as it loses touch with Russian producers and dancers.

2.—BALLET THEATRE

We have recently seen in this country one group of American dancers, Ballet Theatre, under a management that has realised the impossible nature of these conditions and that is making the difficult and plucky effort to fight against them. How difficult the fight will be we can scarcely realise without an accurate knowledge of American labour conditions which make each new production an almost impossibly expensive undertaking, thus preventing much experiment and making it difficult to remedy mistakes. The fight, however, is well worth making, as Ballet Theatre has proved by the fine quality of its dancers.

These young American dancers are magnificently disciplined and splendidly trained from a mechanical point of view. They can perform anything that a choreographer could demand. They have a keen sense of rhythm rather than musical subtlety, accuracy and vitality, but not much lyricism. They possess the ability to " give " with real enthusiasm. They made friends, so to speak, the moment the curtain rose, yet never by unworthy methods. Although they were of diverse races the company had a very positive personality of its own, proving the wisdom of relying on mass personality rather than on the press-created star.

The leading classicist of the company was the Cuban, Alicia Alonso. She has admirable qualities, magnificent feet and legs, great ease and fluidity of movement and a pleasing if elusive personality that requires development. At present it is obvious that she is very much under the influence of Alicia Markova, whose performances she has watched in the same company and whose particular form of dancing suits neither her physique nor essentially Latin temperament. It is perhaps unfair to judge her performance in *Giselle*, choreographically a very poor affair, but the whole interpretation was a sketch of Markova's and entirely lacking in the first act gaiety that can alone form the dramatic contrast to what follows. Her Giselle was doomed from curtain rise. Her finest expression of classicism was in the pas de deux from *Don Quixote*, an extremely fluent piece of work. Physically her chief defect lay in a certain rigidity of back resulting in a forward thrust that may very easily grow into a mannerism. Care on the part of the management in the production of the classics should make valuable use of a very charming artist.

In its leading men Ballet Theatre showed us some truly magnificent athletes, and it is not a coincidence that the great majority of Russian male teachers live in the United States. Outstanding as an artist was the character dancer Michael Kidd, whose work showed both sensibility and intelligence. His Petrouchka was almost all that remained of Fokine's masterpiece in what was a singularly uninspired production. With guidance it could become an outstanding interpretation. As a dancer, Kidd is in the Woizikovski, Shabelevsky, Lazovsky class, but he has gifts that are purely American as he reveals in his own *On Stage,* when he gives a piece of Chaplinesque mime that is a delight. Unlike the majority of performers who can make an audience laugh with ease, Kidd has great restraint. His effects are deliberate, the detail is worked out with great skill, and his charm is undoubted.

John Kriza, the company's classical male dancer, is splendidly equipped technically, magnificently built, and is a gallant partner who should in time find that rare quality the grand manner. He shone in a quantity of rôles, from the rollick-ing sailor in *Fancy Free* to a classical *pas de deux,* but in the classics in general he needs more production and at times there are echoes of Dolin. There can be little doubt that both Dolin and Markova have had a considerable influence on the young American dancers. Both are highly individual and are not such good models to follow, as would be a Danilova or a Wilzak, for instance.

André Eglevsky occupied something of the position of a guest artist, being out-side much of the main repertoire. We first saw this magnificent dancer with de Basil during that dazzling Alhambra season of 1933, and he became a yearly visitor until 1939. We admired the quality of his slow turns in *Les Présages,* his *balon* seen to perfection in Fokine's last masterpiece, *L'Epreuve d'Amour,* and the remarkable lightness with which he handled his height and weight. These same qualities are present to-day with a new found ease that becomes nonchalance at times. Eglevsky is a very considerable dancer. Within certain well defined limits there are none better, but he has yet to master a rôle requiring the slightest subtlety of interpretation. His Blue Bird was a joy in spite of a *batterie* that was not always convincing, but he failed in a remarkable revival of Balanchine's *Apollon-Musagètes* where the young Lifar had been supreme, and he failed totally as Albrecht in *Giselle,* not through the usual faults of commission but through his omission to do anything but dance. His *Sylphides* I personally find outstanding. It may lack the true romantic spirit, but it is danced in so virile a manner that it forms the perfect contrast demanded by the choreography to the dancing of the women, and save for Igor Yuoskevitch I can think of no one at the present day whose dancing stresses that all important point. There is also in his work the im-pression that he takes enormous pleasure in the physical effort of dancing, that the medium is entirely natural to him; that also is rare among contemporary male dancers, especially the classicists.

This joy in the physical aspect of dancing was shown throughout the ranks of these young Americans. Added to the vitality of the country itself one could notice the fact that for years they had been well nourished. There can be no doubt that our own dancers have been struggling against a lack of adequate food and also the lack of sleep of the war years.

Among its solistes Ballet Theatre had a number of young dancers of exceptional promise. Foremost for lyrical quality of the Beryl Grey type was Diana Adams, who should be dancing the classics. She has not only a magnificent line but a feeling for music over and above the rhythmic sense that is common to all. She does not share what is a common characteristic, the overlong holding of a pose that may be highly effective in itself but that cuts into the flow of the music. In that interesting but unsatisfactory ballet, *Graziana,* and in Tudor's essentially lyrical *Jardin Au Lilas,* she reveals herself as an outstanding performer, who with careful handling should make a really distinguished career.

Norma Vaslavina in *Graziana,* as the youngest sister in *Pillar of Fire,* and as the French ballerina in *Gala Performance,* has true gaiety and sparkle, an inner gaiety of the type with which Baronova charmed us as the midinette in *Le Beau Danube* in 1933. Melissa Hayden, a Canadian, has a more exuberant gaiety that she may have to hold in check, though at present it is entirely spontaneous. Her performance in Robbins' brilliant *Interplay* was an outstanding one, not only from a dancing point of view but because it caught the whole spirit of the work. Anna Cesselka showed in the same ballet a talent that should carry her far when she becomes more mature. Muriel Bentley, a character dancer of striking looks and personality, brings a finish to all her work. She is a dancer who thinks and studies detail with meticulous care. At moments she succeeded in making bearable the crude and tedious *Three Virgins and a Devil.* That must rank as an achievement. Barbara Fallis gave style to everything she undertook.

Lucia Chase, the guiding spirit of this fine enterprise and its founder, is in the right rôle a considerable artist, and the right rôle is one in which her very real charm and her acting ability can have full play. Two such rôles were those of the elder sister in *Pillar of Fire,* which could scarcely have been bettered, and in that drab work *Bluebeard,* where almost alone she caught some of the gaiety of Offenbach. In *Les Sylphides* or in *Petrouchka* she is miscast and out of her element. Hugh Laing and Anthony Tudor rank as specialists in the latter's work. It is impossible to place Laing as a dancer. He is perfectly cast in *Pillar of Fire, Jardin Au Lilas* and *Romeo and Juliet,* and it would be difficult to imagine anyone in his place. Tudor himself has no pretentions to being a great dancer. He is beyond a doubt a very remarkable interpreter of the rôles he has assigned himself. In *Jardin Au Lilas* he dominates the scene with a creation that might have stepped out of the pages of de Maupassant, a strong contrast to his well balanced hero in *Pillar of Fire* or the Tybalt in *Romeo and Juliet.*

It is interesting here to note the influence of British ballet on the American scene. Tudor both as choreographer and artistic administrator has a major influence on Ballet Theatre, while Fredera Franklin as *maître de ballet* has a similar influence on the Monte Carlo Ballet—an American Company that has had no recent connection with the municipality.

3.—NORA KAYE

New directions in choreography when they are of a very personal nature often call for a new type of dancer, a specialist who can in a sense collaborate with the choreographer whose creation she is.

When Leonide Massine launched the vogue of symphonic ballet with *Les Présages* (Tchaikovsky Fifth Symphony) he found in Nina Verchinina the perfect " symphonic " dancer, someone who combined Duncanism and ballet to an extraordinary degree. Without her the first movement in *Les Présages* and the second in *Choreartium* (Brahms Fourth Symphony) are left very empty even when a good dancer is entrusted with them. It is always open to discussion whether a narrow specialisation either in choreography or dancing is good for ballet in general. If the work produced is beautiful and significant, then the cause of ballet is well served, always so long as its nature is rightly understood, so long as it is regarded as being something personal and not as a school piece that lends itself to imitation or adaptation. We have seen too many potted symphonies danced by imitation Verchininas.

Much of the early work of Balanchine called for specialised types of dancing and he found admirable interpreters in Lifar *(La Chatte, Apollo)* and in Doubrovska *(Ode)*. Even his later work, such as *Concurrence* and that masterpiece *Cotillon*, required the naive talent of the then unformed Toumanova, Baronova and Riabouchinska to show it to full advantage.

The work of a Fokine or an Ashton can be interpreted by any well equipped classical dancer. De Valois is in a sense a specialist *(Job, Rake's Progress, Prospect Before Us)*, but her work is well within the grasp of the British dancer just as *Petrouchka* is suited to the temperament of the Russian dancer.

The choreography of Antony Tudor calls for a high degree of specialisation, and in order to understand Nora Kaye, the dancer, who is his interpreter *par excellence,* it is first essential to study his masterpiece, *Pillar of Fire,* beyond a doubt one of the great works of the ballet repertoire.

Pillar of Fire tells a story that is far more complicated in print than in action, a story that centres around the emotions of a frustrated woman.

Hagar is the middle of three sisters. The eldest is a precise and rather bitter spinster who stands as a terrifying example to the passionate Hager. The youngest is a flirtatious and over-sexed young minx, every one of whose actions is approved and applauded by the eldest.

Once these three characters have been established the action that follows is clear. Hagar is in love with a steady and somewhat retiring young man who has doubtless not yet declared himself, though the exact relationship is obvious. They are " walking-out " prior to the betrothal in the manner of a small town in the year 1900; the setting of the ballet. The youngest sister out of sheer spite sets her cap at this man and is encouraged by the spinster. He is amused, a little flattered and goes out with her but without any serious intention. It is probably a biting remark by her eldest sister that makes Hagar, now thoroughly overwrought, give herself to the local lady killer. At first she hesitates between disgust, the inherent respectability of her environment, and her longing for love. The struggle and its conflicting motives are very evident. Her surrender brings nothing but shame and disappointment, especially when she realises that it was quite unnecessary, that her sister was acting purely out of caprice and that her intended is faithful. From then on we follow the action on two planes, partly in reality and partly in Hagar's imagining. We see her analyse the family relationship and sort out her views on love. In two dances of extraordinary beauty we assist at a dialogue between Hagar and the man in which everything is argued and explained and mutual recriminations are made. And finally we see the declaration of a noble and understanding love, a true marriage dance that culminates in an apotheosis with the spiritual lovers climbing together up a woodland path and into the unknown future while they lie together in a physical embrace in the wood itself.

There are but three lines by way of programme note, yet every movement is crystal clear. It is significant that Hagar alone is named.

The superficial have objected that this is a psychological subject and that therefore it has no place in ballet, yet there are times when ballet can treat of psychology more vividly than in any other medium (e.g., Helpmann's Freudian commentary on *Hamlet*). In medicine the psychiatrist often finds his first warnings of insanity through a careful analysis of movement. Only if the choreographer had treated the subject from a literary point of view, as a wordless play, would the objection be valid. Tudor has done this, he has treated it as pure ballet from every point of view. All movement flows directly from the music, Schoenberg's *Verklärte Nacht,* and the movement itself is based on an exceedingly close observation of natural gesture disciplined by the classical dance. There is no " pulling of faces," everything depends on the expressiveness of the dancer's body.

It will be seen from this very brief analysis of the choreography the exact demands Tudor makes upon the dancer. She requires a strong classical technique as an essential basis, an absolute understanding of the character, and an altogether exceptional restraint.

In Nora Kaye, so far the sole interpreter of Hagar, Mr Tudor has found his ideal dancer.

Norah Kaye was born in New York of Russian parentage, and was mainly a pupil of Michael Fokine, though to Tudor is obviously due much of her artistic formation. From the moment that the curtain rises on *Pillar of Fire,* she establishes herself as a major artist. We discover her seated on the steps of her house, taut, tormented, a mass of inhibitions. It is obvious from every line in her body that she is on the verge of a brainstorm. And when her sisters emerge she makes the reason abundantly clear. Nora Kaye has been called the Duse of the dance, tempting alliteration admittedly, but the comparison is not too far fetched. It would be difficult to imagine a more expressive back or greater restraint. There are absolutely no frills or ornaments in the choreography, and Norah Kaye is direct in her expression of it. The personality she creates is a tremendous one, but it is always Hagar's and never Nora Kaye as Hagar. I watched a dozen per-

IRENE SKORIK, YOULY ALGAROFF and NATHALIE PHILIPPART

NINA BARONOVA

HAROLD TURNER

BERYL GREY

JULIA FARRON

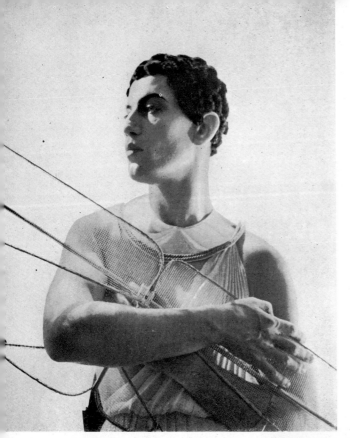

SERGE LIFAR

JEAN BABILEE

formances and the detail that went to the building of the character was extra-ordinary. This was great dancing beyond a doubt.

In Tudor's *Romeo and Juliet,* a ballet to not very suitable music by Delius and consequently a failure, though a not inglorious one—moments in this hour long ballet reach a very high level—Nora Kaye interprets an entirely different type of character. She changes her personality so completely with the assumption of a red wig that it is difficult to recognise in her the tense Hagar or to tell that it is Nora Kaye. There is passion once again and restraint, but it is the girlish passion of a yet unformed character. It is lyrical and as definitely belonging to the Italian Renaissance as Hagar did to the new England of the beginning of the century. The bedroom scene and the dressing of Juliet for her wedding with Paris deserve to survive on their own as complete choreographic poems. Here is magnificent material used by an inspired interpreter.

In Tudor's witty *Gala Performance,* Nora Kaye takes the rôle of the Russian ballerina. She has the necessary technical equipment to make an astringent commentary on the Russian virtuoso. Unfortunately, however, the whole production is treated as a burlesque and aims at catching a laugh rather than a smile. One can realise the broadening effect of playing such a work on tour in front of unsophisticated audiences. The failure here is one of adaptability.

During the season (July-August, 1946) we had an opportunity of seeing Nora Kaye in excerpts from the classics, notably *The Black Swan,* with its notorious thirty-two *fouettés.* Such excerpts introduced into an evening of ballet are disconcerting and can have no real artistic meaning. Those thirty-two *fouettés,* much as I dislike them, have in their context a dramatic significance. Odiles uses them to dazzle the Prince; they are the climax to an act of seduction. Performed in cold blood they are nothing but acrobatics. All this must be admitted before writing of Nora Kaye as a classicist. She has the complete mechanical equipment, but she does not reveal the true classical technique. She stresses the difficulties, underlines them so to speak, with the result that the line is clipped and lacking in the nobility so essential in the classical dance. Those thirty-two *fouettés* are made *sur place* but they are not well executed for all that. It may well be that so essentially an intellectual dancer as Nora Kaye requires a dramatic reason for movement, a definite character to interpret. Her Queen of the Wilis in *Giselle* is dramatically conceived, but again does not fit completely into the classical framework and is mechanical rather than technical. Whether this lack of classical feeling is temperamental and therefore permanent or whether it comes from a lack of adequate production is open to discussion. Personally, I believe it to be temperamental. In Michael Kidd's *Off Stage* she dances a wonderfully complex *pas de deux* based on the classical technique, but here again she is acting a very definite character, a ballerina, and the dance is intended to reveal her type. We see her in private life both before and after the *pas de deux.*

The dancer with a complete width of range is a very rare phenomenon. Karsavina was such a one, to-day Fonteyn approaches completeness. Such dancers are usually the more lyrical classicists. In her own line Nora Kaye is unsurpassed and speaks with magnificent fluency the new choreographic language of Antony Tudor. Her performance as Hagar ranks in my memory among the really great.

CHAPTER XV. — SOME FRENCH DANCERS

THE LIFAR CULT

If dancers are to give anything more than merely competent technical perform-ances, they must have a belief in the management of their company. They must know that they are being watched by someone who understands them and who is ready after the performance with blame or praise. A Diaghileff, a de Valois, a Kochno, or a Lifar, although they have little else in common, can bring out that extra quality in the dancer that the audience feels but that no critic can analyse.

Very recently we have seen a new generation of French dancers. Yvette Chauviré, the outstanding classicist among them, I will write of in some detail For a long time France had given us nothing but a sterile academism. To-day it is different, the spark of creation is there once again. This is largely due to the " Serge Lifar cult " among French dancers, and no other word will describe the influence that he has had. While I disagree profoundly with some of his choreo-graphy, I have a deep admiration for his flair and for the courage with which he has struck away the red tape of Paris Opera conservatism. Serge Lifar was the last of Diaghileff's brilliant creations, one of the most brilliant, and it was only after Diaghileff's death that he came to his full stature as a classical dancer, giving performances in *Giselle* and in the *Blue Bird pas de deux* that remain unforget-table.

As choreographer and maître de ballet of the Paris Opera he gave the dancer a new status, and made an evening of ballet into something fashionable and exciting. The dancers of whom I am writing in this chapter owe everything not only to his direct example but to the atmosphere that he created.

YVETTE CHAUVIRE AS GISELLE

In London in the early summer of 1946, we saw four Giselles: Margot Fonteyn, Alicia Alonso, Yvette Chauviré and Sally Gilmour. The last three performed on the same night. This must surely create a balletic record. Two of those Giselles were outstanding, Margot Fonteyn for her dramatic intensity and Yvette Chauviré for her perfect classicism.

This rôle will always tempt the ballerina; it is the supreme test of her ability as an interpreter, calling for gaïety, simplicity, stark tragedy and then a mood of tenderness as the spirit of the dead girl pleads for her lover, struggling with the curse that has accompanied her suicide's death. Mood follows mood in rapid succession as the period-romantic story unfolds, but the choreographic language calls for the purest classicism, making tremendous demands on the dancer as a technician.

At this stage it is of the utmost importance to distinguish between pure technique and mechanics. Technique is when the mechanics of the dance are used for a particular purpose and are hidden as a consequence. Mechanics belong to the classroom; technique to the stage. If I have not made this distinction previously, it is because it is only very recently that we have seen a number of dancers flawless from a mechanical point of view who have quite erroneously been pointed out as models of pure classical technique. Trafilova has ever been my model of the classical dancer. No one could conceal her mechanics more completely. Camille Schwarz in the Blue Bird *pas de deux* and Nora Kaye in the Black Swan *pas de deux* do not reveal a true classical technique but merely the mechanics of such a technique laid bare. This is a distinction that must be thoroughly understood in the interests of the true classical dance. Artistry is yet another matter over and above any consideration of technique.

Yvette Chauviré was seen in a production of *Giselle* that in many particulars would have disgraced the Women's Institute at Much-Binding-on-the-March.

Yet her performance was the greatest and most moving I have seen since Pavlova's and I am convinced it was more impersonal and within the period classical framework. The very essence of this performance was its period feeling. Chauviré made one see Giselle as a contemporary, through the eyes of those great romantic lithographers, Brandard and Chalon. She achieved something else; for the first time the music seemed not only suitable but genuinely moving. One had the impression that this was how its creator Grisi must have danced. Many among the greatest Giselles have put more into it than music or period demanded, have seemed conscious of the greatness of the opportunity, and what is more significant have been cradled as artists in Fokine's neo-romanticism. *Les Sylphides* is after all a possible re-statement of the second act of *Giselle,* a truly romanticised re-statement in which the period classical-romantic conventions have no place. The majority of dancers to-day in *Swan Lake* are definitely post-Fokine in their attack. One is conscious that they have danced *Les Sylphides*. Yvette Chauviré is the complete classicist. Her mime is infinitely moving and her scene of insanity is superb, but it is in her second act that she is quite unsurpassed. Apart from the dramatic element the sheer effortless beauty of her line is deeply moving. She gives the feeling of holding so much in reserve which is of the very essence of true classicism.

Unfortunately it was impossible for Londoners during that Cambridge Theatre season to judge of Chauviré's range as a dancer or of her artistry in general. Her Giselle remains a model for every dancer of this generation, an inspiring model devoid of the slightest mannerism.

The emergence of the French dancer is still a surprise. Their appearance in the general ballet scene has happened recently after the bulk of this book was written. The formation of Chauviré was no accident. She has been followed by Jeanmaire, Charrat, Tcherina, Marchand, and many others. There is a creative vitality in France that has not existed for half a century.

RENÉE JEANMAIRE

In Yvette Chauviré Serge Lifar gave us one of the greatest classical ballerinas of the day. In Renée Jeanmaire he has produced an inspired classical soubrette, heroine of *Coppelia* and *La Fille Mal Gardée*. Jeanmaire is a dancer of extraordinary intelligence and, to her, dancing is clearly a glorious adventure. In such rôles as the *fouetté*-turning schoolgirl in *Graduation Ball* she can give life to what has become a rather tedious commonplace, because these *fouettés* are in fact the expression of her own gaiety. It is a pity that when she appeared with Colonel de Basil's Russian Ballet she was so often seriously miscast. Anyone fortunate enough to have seen her in Lifar's *Aubade,* specially created for her, or in Kniaseff's *Piccoli,* will understand the unique quality of this dancer. She has the gift of mocking her audience, treating them not with contempt, but with an attitude of amused flirtation. Yet though she has so often been miscast she has been able to show considerable versatility. Her Aurora has enormous dignity, the soubrette is forgotten, and she makes her entrance in the grand manner. One feels that every inch of her body is directly controlled by her brain, which in ballet means personality, and Jeanmaire is an outstanding personality. As the temptress in Lichine's *Prodigal Son* she builds a strong dramatic characterisation with remarkable success.

THE CHAMPS-ELYSEES AND ROLAND PETIT GROUPS :

VYROUBOVA, CHARRAT, MARCHAND, PHILIPPART

It is rare for a dancer to arrive unheralded and unknown and to receive a five minute ovation from her audience. Nina Vyroubova was to have appeared as ballerina of the *Ballets des Champs Elysées* for their season at the Winter Garden Theatre in 1947. *La Sylphide* had been specially revived for her by Boris Kochno, but on the eve of the London première she was operated on for appendicitis and she did not make an appearance until the last performance but one of the season, having arrived from Paris that afternoon by 'plane.

It was immediately obvious why Boris Kochno had been inspired to revive *La Sylphide*. Without Vyroubova it was a quaint museum piece. She made it into something living by the extraordinary sense of atmosphere she was able to convey.

Vyroubova has a strong classical technique allied to that rare quality also possessed by Riabouchinska and Markova of being able to move one deeply by the attribute of lightness.

The differences between a Chauviré, a Jeanmaire, and a Vyroubova, all trained in the Russian classical school, are differences of physique and temperament, but they are also conscious differences of presentation, as can be clearly seen when one of these dancers steps out of her speciality, as did Chauviré in *Chota Roustaveli,* or Jeanmaire in *Les Sylphides*. All are classical, but within classicism there is scope for the nostalgic romanticism of a Vyroubova, the dramatic romanticism of a Chauviré, and the Gallic wit and sparkle of a Jeanmaire.

Two other dancers who must be mentioned are Janine Charrat and Colette Marchand. Charrat is essentially a choreographer, a very individual dancer, and therefore an exception to what I write below. She has undoubtedly, as her technique shows, been much influenced by the dancing of the East, her hands and arms have an expressiveness outside the classical ballet framework. Everything that she does, so long as it is not classical, is intensely interesting. Colette Marchand is a pure classicist from the Opéra school, but with the lovely line of the Russians and the figure of a Tanagra statuette. She has a quality that, added to experience, will carry her far.

Each one of these dancers can invade the other's territory, as Elssler did Taglioni's. It is this question of presentation that is so important and that can only be imparted by a teacher with a large stage experience. It lies in musical phrasing, in the use of the head and eyes, and in the ability to create certain optical illusions. I have for instance seen Kniaseff demonstrate the illusion of enormous elevation without leaving the ground. This presentation is the top dressing of technique and it is here that the young French dancer excels. Boris Kniaseff, teacher of Chauviré, Jeanmaire, and in part of Vyroubova, and the serenely classical Iréne Skorik, the most Russian in style of these four, has played a great rôle in the contemporary French dance. He has not only given these dancers a strong technique but has developed each one along her own particular lines.

IRENE SKORIK

There is one young dancer whose position as ballerina of a highly creative company singles out for separate treatment. Irène Skorik has been ballerina of the Champs-Elysées company since its inception. Her first season she was promising but immature, her next season she was overcome by a serious illness, and only now have we had an opportunity of seeing what a sensitive and individual artist she has become. Only two or three dancers in a generation reach a completeness in which there is perfect balance between mind, spirit and body. Irène Skorik has not yet attained such completeness—she may never do so—but she is nevertheless one of the most interesting dancers developed by one of the most interesting companies since Diaghileff's day.

In the classical repertoire her most sustained characterisation has been that of La Sylphide. Vyroubova recreated the rôle and was so perfectly cast that her performance remains memorable. Skorik, however, has given it a more moving interpretation, her sylph is both more woman and more *terre à terre*. There is none of the lightness that Gautier associated with Taglioni and that we saw in Vyroubova, there is instead a display of strong emotion all the more effective for being held in reserve. This sylph is a thwarted creature who cannot love as other mortals. I would rank the performance, and I saw it a dozen times, as one of the most touching I have ever seen, and the music was no help.

Surprisingly enough, Skorik's Swanhilda had a gaiety that I should never have suspected and a few moments of great distinction, there where the suspected doll pretends to gain life.

In her classical *pas de deux,* Skorik is often strangely clumsy in spite of the beauty of her line, but once again what distinguishes her is the warm response to the music of Tchaikovsky. She is not content merely to dazzle, she seeks to interpret, and as yet cannot fully control herself, giving an appearance of weight that does not actually exist. Equally striking is the integrity of her work. She does not modify technique to create an impression of ease or virtuosity in the manner of so many dancers of the new American school whose apparent fluency so easily carries an audience with it. Yet I would rank her partial failure higher than their seeming success. There is about her work a warmth and humanity that must move one, there is that mysterious Mona Lisa smile that gives one the impression that she is possessed of a secret, of something that she is striving to understand, partly in ecstasy, partly perplexed.

It is only when writing of a Chauviré or a Fonteyn, those rare " complete " artists, that one is on safe grounds. Otherwise criticism can only be extremely subjective, depending on a taste that cannot be argued about though it can be disagreed with. That is so in the case of this young Franco-Russian dancer who has moved me for the reasons I have tried to convey. She may take a direction that will spoil this impression of extreme sensitivity or she may find herself completely and rank with the very few. Whatever happens, I shall remember and be grateful for the suffering of La Sylphide, the gaiety of Swanhilda, and the spirit that Tchaikovsky inspired.

THREE MALE DANCERS :

BABILEE, SKOURATOFF, KALIOUJNY

A dancer who has made an enormous impression is Jean Babilée. He has danced both the classics and modern works specially composed around his personality. Babilée is temperamental and uneven, so that in such a brilliant virtuoso piece as the Blue Bird he gives one astonishing performance to several that could be a very great deal better. It is in works created for him, such as *Le Jeune Homme et la Mort, Le Rendezvous* and *Jeux de Cartes* that we see the true artist, and indeed his personality is so closely associated with these ballets that it is difficult to tell what their value choreographically would be without him.

He is a dancer who lends himself to " personal " choreography as does his very brilliant partner, Nathalie Philippart, who, like Nina Verchinina and Nora Kaye, excels in work that has been created for and by her. This team of highly individual dancers revolve very much round the personality of Roland Petit himself as an excellent dancer and a considerable artist in the right rôle. His performance in *Les Forains* is unforgettable.

Apart from the Champs-Élysées group there are many male dancers from France with a truly masculine approach to their work, among them the altogether phenomenal Kalioujny, who is as fine a classicist as a character dancer; Emile Audran, Youly Algaroff, and the intensely musical Vladimir Skouratoff, potentially one of the finest romantic dancers of our day and one of the few to distinguish between true romanticism and sloppy sentimentality.